AMERICAN VOICES

GERMAN AMERICANS

AMERICAN VOICES

GERMAN AMERICANS

by **Bernard A. Cook**
and **Rosemary Petralle Cook**

Rourke Corporation, Inc.
Vero Beach, Florida 32964

Cover photo: David Fowler

∞The paper used in this book conforms to the American National Standard for Permanence of Paper for Printed Library Materials, Z39.48-1984.

Library of Congress Cataloging-in-Publication Data
Cook, Bernard A.
  German Americans/by Bernard A. Cook and
Rosemary Petralle Cook.
    p.   cm.—(American voices)
  Includes bibliographical references and index.
  Summary: Discusses Germans who have
immigrated to the United States, their reasons for
coming, where they have settled, and how they have
contributed to their new country.
  ISBN 0-86593-140-2
  1. German Americans—Juvenile literature.
[1. German Americans.] I. Cook, Rosemary Petralle.
1943-   . II. Title. III. Series.
E184.G3C653   1991   91-15030
973'.0431—dc20   CIP
                                              AC

PRINTED IN THE UNITED STATES OF AMERICA

CONTENTS

AMERICAN VOICES

GERMAN AMERICANS

THE GERMANS

IN NORTH AMERICA

More than seven million Germans came to the United States. Today, 52 million Americans, nearly a quarter of the population, are descendants of German-speaking immigrants. Although many Americans possess ancestors of diverse ethnic backgrounds, Americans who claim German descent outnumber the 43.7 million Americans who trace their ancestry to Ireland and the 40 million who trace their ancestry to England. This makes German Americans the largest European ethnic group in the United States. In Canada, people of German descent constitute the largest group after the French and English: 1.1 million Canadians, approximately 6.3 percent of the population, are of German descent.

So many Americans have German roots, in fact, that it is difficult to speak of a distinct German ethnic group in the United States today. Most Americans who call themselves German today are separated from their immigrant ancestors by at least two generations.

MANY HOMELANDS, ONE LANGUAGE

German-speaking people began to arrive in America more than three hundred years ago, before there was a single German country. Lacking political unity, they were united by their culture and their language. At first it was especially the language that distinguished German immigrants from their

British counterparts. At the end of the American Revolutionary War, it was even suggested that German be made the official language of the new country, to set it apart from Britain. At that time, of the approximately 3 million inhabitants of the thirteen original states, 225,000 were of German descent.

As time went on, new arrivals from Germany were set apart by their language; those who had been in the new country longer were learning English. Some German communities attempted to preserve their language through German-language newspapers and cultural activities. English, however, remained the official tongue, and most German immigrants made the effort to learn English and were able to get by rather quickly.

Germans nevertheless contributed many familiar words to the English language, such as *blitz*, *kaffeeklatsch*, *kindergarten*, *pretzel*, *sauerkraut*, and *wiener*. The language of the Germans who came to America is still recognizable in many family names and place names in America. Müller (meaning "miller"), Schmidt (from *Schmied*, or "smith"), Koch (cook), Radermacher (wheel maker), Wassermann (waterman), Kaufmann (merchant), Bauer (peasant), and many other family names reveal the occupations of past German ancestors. Family names such as Rosenthal (rose valley), Thalheim (valley home), Grunwald (green woods), and Schwarzenberg (black mountain) refer to places. Many towns in the United States and Canada are named after places in Germany or Germans: Heidelberg, Mississippi; Potsdam, New York; Berlin, Wisconsin; Bismarck, North Dakota; Bernardsdorf, Massachusetts; Humboldt, Saskatchewan; and Rhineland, Manitoba, are only some of them.

VALUES: HEARTH, HOME, HARD WORK

German culture centered on the family. A simple life revolving around the home was the German idea of happiness.

Germans had a strong sense of family duty and obligation. They revered their ancestors and were concerned about the sort of legacy they would leave to their children. They believed in learning, hard work, and persistence. They were loyal to friends and wanted to be regarded as productive members of the community. Many Germans had another characteristic, frugality: They were careful about spending money and they avoided wastefulness.

Good times, good friends, and good fun are shared at the Festival of American Folklife in Washington, D.C.

3

GEMÜTLICHKEIT: A LOVE OF LIFE

Even though Germans worked hard and were very serious, they believed in enjoying life. The German outlook on life was in some ways similar to the traditional Puritanism of their British-born neighbors, but in other ways it was quite different. Both groups valued industriousness—the traditional Puritan "work ethic." The Puritans, however, were as a whole rather dour, having a reputation for looking askance at pleasure and merriment.

Germans, on the other hand, loved to eat and drink, enjoyed company, and liked entertainment. This taste for sharing good times with others, called *Gemütlichkeit*, pervaded their daily lives. For example, most Germans went to church, but after church they spent the rest of the day playing outdoor games and socializing. As a result, Germans helped to transform Sunday in America into a day of rest and enjoyment.

TRADITIONS: HOLIDAYS, FOOD, MUSIC

The Germans' love of life can also be seen in the many traditions they introduced to America. The celebration of the Christmas holiday with the Christmas tree, gift giving, good food, and family togetherness was largely German in origin. The special New Year celebration was also introduced by German immigrants, and with it, their national drink, beer. Before the middle of the nineteenth century, beer was not often found in America. The Germans established breweries to produce their beverage and built beer gardens as places to socialize.

Along with beer, the Germans brought their taste for a wide variety of foods: sausage, roast meat and gravy, potatoes, cabbage, and pastries of all sorts. Many of these dishes have come to be considered typically "American": Both the hot dog (Frankfurter) and the hamburger (from Hamburg) were German culinary contributions to their new country.

Delectable desserts include (from left) funnel cake, shoofly pie, and dried apple schnitz. These were made in Lancaster County, Pennsylvania.

The German emphasis upon enjoyment had other facets. They brought with them a love of music. Bands and singing were popular at German social gatherings. Beer halls and beer gardens were places not only for meeting acquaintances, engaging in friendly talk, and discussing political issues, but also for singing and sometimes dancing. The polka and waltz were favorite dances of the Germans, as well as of other central Europeans. Besides informal and spontaneous singing, German immigrants set up choral societies and orchestras. They brought to America their folk music, but also the music of their great composers. Germans founded many of the great symphony orchestras of North America. They also established amateur theaters in their communities. German athletic societies, called *Turnvereine* (turn′fah•rī•nah), encouraged physical fitness and qualities of honor and comradeship.

5

AN INDEPENDENT SPIRIT: RELIGIOUS BELIEFS

Germans also influenced the religious culture of America. After the Thirty Years' War (1618-1648)—a struggle for dominion in which Protestant princes of the German states aligned against the Habsburg powers of Austria and Spain, led by the Catholic Holy Roman emperor Ferdinand II—only Catholics, Lutherans, and Calvinists were tolerated in Germany. People who did not conform to these three religions were harassed or were forced to emigrate. These groups contributed to the interesting diversity of American society, and some still constitute separate communities in which old ways and values are preserved.

Many colonial Germans were members of the dissident sects. One of the first groups was the German Baptist Brethren, known as the Dunkers, from the word *tunken*, meaning "to immerse." This name referred to the Dunkers' practice of immersing the entire body in water during the rite of baptism. They settled in Germantown, Pennsylvania, in 1729.

Other large groups were the Amish and Mennonites, who also settled in Pennsylvania. The Mennonites stressed a simple and peaceful way of life, and Mennonite communities across the United States and Canada continue their traditions of simplicity, peace, and justice to this day.

The Amish, named after their founder, Jacob Ammann (or Amen), were originally a sect of the Mennonites that separated to lead more austere lives. Today, they live only in Pennsylvania, the Midwest, and Canada, where they isolate themselves in rural communities. Because of their religious convictions, they refuse to use electricity or telephones, drive cars, dress in fashionable clothing, or send their children to public schools. Sometimes the Amish are referred to as the Pennsylvania Dutch, but they are German. (The "Dutch" does not mean Dutch at all, but comes from the German word *deutsch*, which means German.) Although they usually know English, the Amish continue to speak German in their religious services, in their schools, and among themselves. Between 1800 and the 1920's, most German immigrants were Catholics or members of one of the two largest German Protestant groups, Lutherans and Calvinists. Half of the German immigrants who came to America after 1800 were Catholic. German immigration significantly increased the Catholic proportion of America's population, but the American Lutheran and the Evangelical and Reformed churches have their roots in Germany as well. After Adolf Hitler came to power in Germany in 1933, he persecuted the Jewish people, interning them in concentration camps, where they were forced into hard labor, tortured, starved, and murdered. Many Jews fled Germany, and more than 140,000 emigrated to the United States. A number of them were outstanding scientists, intellectuals, and artists, and they made significant contributions to American education, science, and culture.

TODAY'S GERMAN AMERICAN

German Americans in most instances rapidly dispersed throughout the country and assimilated into the cultural mainstream of America. Today "German American" means having ancestors who were mainly German, and 23 percent of the U.S. population falls into this category. These people are spread throughout the country and are found in all social classes and occupations. On average, they have experienced a degree of economic success, and in their attitudes they tend to be conservative. Among the German Americans there is a slightly higher number of married people than the national average, a lower rate of unemployment, and a higher level of education.

In one category, however, they stand out. A higher percentage of German Americans than any other national group are farmers. German characteristics are preserved in the small German farming communities where so many Germans settled, and in some neighborhoods of the cities and towns of the Midwest. Though today most German Americans have largely assimilated, they continue to contribute much to the mosaic of modern American life.

THE COMMUNITY

German-American communities were characterized not only by industriousness, orderliness, and seriousness, but also by a strong sense of group identity. German rural communities in the Midwest and German farms tended to be well kept, well managed, and very clean. German communities were established in many cities as well, and in some Midwestern cities they were so pronounced that they gave a German character to the entire city.

With the passage of many years, it became difficult for Germans living in urban environments to isolate themselves and avoid a gradual process of assimilation. As a result, most urban German communities have disappeared, victims of mobility and the "melting pot." Little remains of the once-active and influential German-language newspapers, and German-American organizations are numerically insignificant. When the Germans arrived as immigrants, however, they did form distinct communities—both in the city and in the country.

A CONVIVIAL PEOPLE

The German poet Johann Wolfgang von Goethe spelled out the German formula for a full life: work during the day followed by socializing in the evening; weeks of toil interspersed with festivals and fun. The Germans loved to share good times with their fellow Germans, and this personality trait made its mark on the German community. Germans transformed Sundays in America into social occasions, and they brought with them their love of special

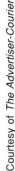

Children join in the fun during the Maifest activities in Hermann, Missouri.

holidays, public gathering places, and clubs. Public parks, for example, are a prominent feature of cities where large numbers of Germans settled.

German saloons also served as centers for community life. They were respectable, well-lit places, welcoming the whole family. There, friends and neighbors could get together for friendly card games, political discussions, and union meetings. The beer halls were often gigantic community centers. Some of the largest in New York's Bowery could accommodate up to three thousand people. Some had glass roofs to let in the sun and to protect patrons from bad weather. They had fixed

10

wooden tables which extended from one end of the hall to the other, with wooden benches instead of chairs. Families, including babies, occupied whole tables.

ORGANIZATIONS FOR ALL OCCASIONS

Considering the German tendency to socialize, it is not surprising that clubs and organizations characterized German community life. There were clubs for every interest, for men and women, young and old. The club, particularly for non-religious Germans, became a focal point for social life. Germans founded physical fitness societies called *Turnvereine*, Masonic and Odd Fellows lodges, and special societies such as the Sons of Hermann, named after the German tribal leader whose warriors defeated three Roman legions in A.D. 9. Mutual aid societies called *Unterstützungsvereine*, which resembled insurance companies, were numerous. Members paid monthly dues, and in case of sickness or death, a family received assistance. In 1915, Chicago, Milwaukee, New York, and Philadelphia each had more than two hundred German-American clubs.

Germans loved to sing. Their singing societies, or *Gesangvereine*, helped to pass on German songs to the younger generation. Their popularity can be seen from a 1900 competition in Brooklyn, which brought together six thousand singers from 174 German choral groups.

In addition to singing societies, Germans organized small groups to perform classical music. These groups and their members were often instrumental in the establishment of symphony orchestras. Philadelphia, because of the influence of its German community, became the first American city with a symphony orchestra.

Besides singing societies and musical groups, German theaters were established in the nineteenth century wherever Germans gathered in the United States. The first major

German-language theater opened in New York in 1840. Professional German theaters thrived in Cincinnati, Chicago, Philadelphia, St. Paul, and Milwaukee. More informal theater groups were set up elsewhere. Friedrich Schiller's *William Tell*, which depicted an individual struggling against tyranny, was one of the most popular plays. It is still performed in German every year in New Glarus, Wisconsin.

There were fifty-eight German women's organizations in St. Louis in 1911. The traditional role assigned to women in the German community was characterized by the motto *Kirche, Kinder, und Küche*, or "Church, Children, and Kitchen." To this must be added the afternoon or evening spent at the *Damenverein* (women's club) playing pinochle, lotto, or euchre.

GERMANS IN THE CITY

By 1850, a German district known as "Kleindeutschland," or "Little Germany," had developed in New York. Until the Civil War, approximately two-thirds of the city's Germans lived there. German was almost exclusively spoken, and the shops were almost all owned by Germans. There were German churches, schools, a German theater, and a German library. The situation was the same in Milwaukee, where a Dane in the 1850's said that many Germans never left their German neighborhoods and did not learn to speak English. In St. Louis only a third of the city's Germans lived in predominantly German wards. Still, the Little Germanies of many cities survived and even flourished throughout the nineteenth century, serving as cultural focal points for Germans who lived in more ethnically diverse neighborhoods.

THE EVOLUTION OF CINCINNATI

Cincinnati was one of the Midwestern cities that had a large German community and a distinct German character. In the

1980 U.S. census, Ohio ranked third among states in its percentage of people of German ancestry. Cincinnati, 45 percent of whose citizens claimed to be German Americans, exceeded the Ohio average by 5 percent. Although the city's German community has been largely absorbed into a general American culture, remnants of its once-thriving German community are still present.

Cincinnati was one of the points on the nineteenth century "German triangle," which it formed with St. Louis and Milwaukee. The first Germans came to the Cincinnati area in 1795, but they constituted only 5 percent of the town's population in 1820. These early Germans served as a magnet. By 1860, 30 percent of the growing city's population was German-born, and by 1890, 57.4 percent of its people were of German background. The hills, the river, and the climate made German immigrants feel at home. Rather than being assimilated by Cincinnati, the mass of new German citizens transformed Cincinnati.

German immigrants in Cincinnati at first congregated in an area across the Miami-Erie canal (now Central Parkway), which was called "Over the Rhine." The area contained small, neat, frame-and-brick houses, flush with the sidewalk. In the fenced backyards, the industrious and frugal Germans grew vegetables. The other side of the German character was present as well. German love of beauty could be seen in the flower gardens and scrubbed steps and sidewalks. *Gemütlichkeit*, the German bent for sociability, was evident in the beer gardens, open-air markets, churches, theaters, and clubs of every sort. After work and on Sundays, German men went to taverns, where they played euchre, skat, and pinochle, or brought their families to open, airy beer gardens to listen to music. Their sense of family and community was expressed in the continual celebration of name days and anniversaries and in the activities of their organizations.

By 1900, Germans lived throughout the city, but the "Over the Rhine" area remained an important social and cultural center. It was home to German musical societies, theaters, clubs, libraries, and newspapers. German Americans produced plays in German not only to amuse themselves but also to keep alive their knowledge of the German language and culture. There were two major German-language daily newspapers, which, in 1914, had a combined circulation of 92,000.

In 1914, there were one hundred German organizations in Cincinnati. Among them were twelve singing societies, thirteen cultural organizations, fifty-nine mutual aid societies, seven charitable organizations, and three large *Turnvereine*. The most successful of the American *Turnvereine* was organized in Cincinnati by Friedrich Hecker in 1848. A Turner Hall was built, and a national publication, *Die Turnzeitung*, was founded. The *Turnvereine* were open to boys and girls for gymnastic exercises and had women's branches. For their older male members, they were largely social clubs. The *Turnverein*, the Deutsche Pionier-Verein, and the German-American Alliance served as focal points for the maintenance of German culture and traditions in Cincinnati. The German founder of the *Turnverein*, Friedrich Jahn, was honored by a statue in Cincinnati's Inwood Park. Students in the public schools of Cincinnati not only had the opportunity to learn German from German-speaking teachers but also, from 1840 until 1917, could choose to attend classes taught in German. This program was destroyed by the anti-German hysteria which swept Cincinnati and much of North America when the United States declared war on Germany in 1917. The bilingual classes were terminated and the teachers fired.

Until World War I, Germans were actively sought by Canadian businessmen as skilled immigrant workers. However, when the war erupted in 1914, many Germans were interned, and their property was confiscated and never returned. The use of the German language was sometimes prohibited. As a result of prejudice and harassment, six thousand Mennonites, whose ancestors had earlier sought refuge in Canada, moved to Latin America. Americans who did not identify themselves as German descendants often feared a group now considered barbaric and violent, and German Americans were labeled "Huns."

Hatred of the German "Huns"—and, as a result, of German Americans—was widespread. In Cincinnati, public meetings conducted in German were outlawed, and German songs could not be sung. Street names were changed. The entire collection of German books was taken out of circulation and moved to the basement of the library. The Jahn statue was repeatedly vandalized, and German Americans were tarred and feathered; two were almost lynched.

The German-American community in Cincinnati survived but was not unscathed. German ethnicity became subdued. The means by which German culture could be preserved and transmitted were destroyed or limited. There were almost as many members of German organizations in the city in 1930 as there had been in 1914, but the surviving societies no longer enlivened a vibrant German community. One-third of the city's fifteen German-language newspapers and journals ceased publication. The singing societies reorganized at the end of the war, but a German play was not produced again until 1925. German books were not put on the library shelves again until 1921. Students could not study German in school until 1926, and then only in high school. Finally, when Prohibition went into effect in 1920, German-American owners of breweries were prevented from manufacturing or selling beer, and an important cultural institution in the German-American community, the family beer garden, was destroyed.

The German heritage increasingly became a private matter,

values to be shared and transmitted by families, or at most by religious organizations or small societies. The language was lost. German Americans became "invisible" ethnics. German Americans have demonstrated their loyalty to America. Today, with democracy flourishing in a united and dynamic Germany, most German Americans proudly acknowledge their heritage.

LIFE IN THE COUNTRY

The German tradition has probably survived to a greater degree in rural areas. In 1870, 27 percent of the German Americans were farmers. Like other American farmers, most German-American farming families lived on typically isolated individual farms. If the Germans did not re-create the typical farming villages of Germany, they were often drawn to areas

Courtesy of *The Advertiser-Courier*

German Americans march in "The Hungry Five" band during a recent Maifest celebration in Hermann, Missouri.

where other Germans had settled or were settling. The presence of nearby German urban communities or heavily German market towns also served as a magnets for German farmers.

One example of a German rural community where aspects of German culture still persist is Hermann, Missouri. Founded by German immigrants in 1837, it had a population of 450 within two years. It became famous for its vineyards, and wine is still produced in the area. In 1848, a theater guild began presenting plays in German every Sunday. Rural conservatism and stability helped to preserve values and behavior. Today the town promotes its cultural background as a means of attracting tourists to its commercialized festivals. Many people in St. Louis with German roots find much to enjoy and to identify with in Hermann.

GERMAN CANADIANS

Most German Canadians, while retaining aspects of their culture, have also assimilated into a generic Canadian culture. The bulk of German-speaking people who immigrated to Canada did not come to Canada from Germany proper. In the case of the Hutterites and some of the Mennonites, they came from Russia, to which their ancestors had immigrated earlier. The Germans who came to Canada were culturally diverse. Most German Canadians today belong to the principal Protestant churches, but approximately 25 percent are Catholic, and 9 percent are Mennonites or Hutterites.

Canadian Germans, like their counterparts in the United States, fostered a rich club and cultural life. The German Benevolent Society, founded in 1835, and the Germania Club, founded in 1864, still exist. In 1951, the Trans-Canada Alliance of German Canadians was founded to promote the preservation of the culture of German Canadians. One of the oldest of Canada's musical organizations, Quebec's Harmonic

Society, was founded in 1820 by the German Henri Glackemeyer. The first German newspaper in Canada, the *Halifax Zeitung*, was established in the 1780's. Today there are still two major German-language newspapers, and German-language broadcasts can be heard on some privately owned radio stations. In Kitchener, Ontario (which was called Berlin until the name was changed in a wave of anti-German feeling during World War I), Canadian Germans continue to hold one of the most famous German festivals, the Oktoberfest, a celebration of harvest and bounty.

GERMAN-AMERICAN COMMUNITIES TODAY

Today, in Canada and in the United States, people of German heritage are regarded as an important and valuable element of the national community, but few think of themselves specifically as members of German-American communities. Instead, most German Americans see themselves as part of a larger community of "middle Americans."

GERMANY

Today German is spoken in Germany, Austria, part of Switzerland, part of Belgium, and Liechtenstein. Most people in Luxembourg speak German in addition to their own dialect, and it is spoken by many people at home in Alsace in eastern France. The region now called Germany was the homeland to most ancestors of German Americans. It is bordered by nine countries: on the north by Denmark; on the west by The Netherlands, Belgium, Luxembourg, and France; on the south by Switzerland and Austria; and on the east by Czechoslovakia and Poland.

HISTORY

When the first Germans came to America, there was not a single German state or country. Before Germany was invaded by the armies of Napoleon, there were more than three hundred German states loosely tied together in what was called the Holy Roman Empire. The leader of this hodgepodge of states was the emperor, who lived in Vienna, but he was mostly a figurehead. Germans were primarily united by their language and a generally shared culture.

Napoleon, after he had overwhelmed his German opponents, redrew the map of Germany. When he was finally defeated, the peace conference which met at Vienna did not restore all of the old German states, but there were still thirty-nine German states. They included kingdoms such as Prussia, Bavaria, Württemberg, and Saxony; the German part of the Austrian Empire; principalities and duchies, such as Hesse and Baden; and even independent city-states, such as Frankfurt and

Hamburg. Germany was not united until 1871.

The state of Prussia—known for its discipline and militarism and led by its chief minister, Otto von Bismarck—successfully challenged Austria's claim to be the leading German state. Through three short wars, Prussia defeated Austria and excluded it from Germany, united the other German states under Prussian leadership, and seized Alsace and Lorraine from France. The German Empire was proclaimed on January 18, 1871, with the Prussian king, Wilhelm, as its *Kaiser*, or emperor.

The unification of Germany was followed by intense economic development. Increasingly, Germany's agricultural character was overshadowed by the growth of cities and the advance of industrialization. By 1900, Germany surpassed Great Britain in the production of iron and steel, a key economic indicator at the time. As Germany grew economically, a new kaiser came to the helm. He was Wilhelm II, the arrogant grandson of the first kaiser.

Wilhelm II lacked the basic moderation of Bismarck, who was satisfied with the boundaries of the Germany that he had united. The young kaiser wanted Germany to become a world power. He fired Bismarck in 1890 and embarked on an adventurous and aggressive foreign policy. Partly because of the kaiser's lack of restraint and the misguided policies of his advisers, Germany by 1914 was confronted by a hostile alliance of Russia and France. Great Britain, though not a formal ally of the French and Russians, had been drawn toward them out of fear of Germany. Believing that a war was inevitable, some German leaders pressed Austria-Hungary to respond vigorously to the June, 1914, assassination of Archduke Franz Ferdinand, the heir to the Austrian throne. When Russia mobilized its forces, Germany launched World War I—which unexpectedly lasted for four years. Two million German soldiers died in battle, and finally an exhausted

Germany collapsed.

Although a new republican government, the Weimar Republic, had replaced the kaiser at the end of the war, the victorious Allies imposed a harsh settlement, the Treaty of Versailles, upon Germany. A demagogue, Adolf Hitler, was able to convince many Germans that the Allies and domestic German traitors, particularly the Jews and the socialists, were responsible for the sufferings that Germany had experienced. The Great Depression, which caused massive unemployment in Germany, particularly aided Hitler. His National Socialist Party—the Nazis—became the largest party in Germany, and he was appointed chancellor, or prime minister, on January 30, 1933. Hitler quickly outlawed all other political parties and transformed Germany into a totalitarian state. In his effort to make Germany dominant in Europe, he launched World War II, which ultimately led to the destruction of his regime and his country.

After World War II, Germany was occupied and divided into two separate German states, communist East Germany, and democratic West Germany. In 1990, Germany was reunited into a single country, but it is a country with considerable physical and cultural diversity.

THE LAND

Germany stretches from the flat, marshy shores of the North Sea and the sand dunes of the Baltic Sea, through the sandy pine forests of Brandenburg and the rolling hills and low mountains of central Germany, to the Alps, which rise near Germany's southern frontiers with Austria and Switzerland. There are five main geographical regions: the low and almost flat North German Plain, the Central Highlands, the South German Hills, the Black Forest, and the Bavarian Alps.

The North German Plain is drained by broad rivers which flow northward to the North and Baltic Seas. The rivers are

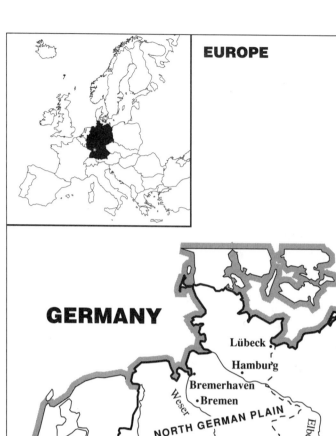

EUROPE

GERMANY

Lübeck

Hamburg

Bremerhaven

Bremen

Weser

NORTH GERMAN PLAIN

Elbe

Berlin ✪

Oder

Hanover

Ems

Weser

Leipzig

Weimar

Dresden

Chemnitz

Elbe

Oder

Dusseldorf

Cologne

Rhine

Marburg

Bonn ✪

CENTRAL HIGHLANDS

Frankfurt

Rhine

Heidelberg

BLACK FOREST

Stuttgart

SOUTH GERMAN HILLS

Freiburg

Danube

Munich
(München)

Danube

BAVARIAN ALPS

– – – Old border
between
East and West
Germany

the Elbe, Ems, Oder, Rhine, and Weser. Before reaching the North Sea, the Rhine flows through The Netherlands. Germany's great port of Hamburg lies on the Elbe; the lesser port of Bremen is on the Weser. The Spree, a tributary of the Elbe, flows through the capital of Germany, Berlin, which is surrounded by the state of Brandenburg. This section of Germany was formerly known as Prussia. Much of the border between Germany and Poland is formed by the Oder River and its tributary, the Neisse. The soil of the river valleys is fertile, but the land between them is largely sand and gravel, better suited for forests than farms.

The Central Highlands is an area of steep and narrow valleys. The famous and beautiful gorges of the Rhine are located there. Much of the land outside the valleys is mountainous and rocky. The Harz Mountains and the Thuringian Forest of this region have some peaks of more than 3,000 feet. Weimar, made famous by Johann Wolfgang von Goethe, and the eastern city of Chemnitz are also in this region.

This South German Hills area is broken by a series of ridges that run from the southwest to the northeast. The lowlands of this region contain some of Germany's best farmland. The South German Hills are drained by the Rhine and its tributaries, the Main and the Necker, as well as the Danube, the only major German river, which flows to the east and then south. Frankfurt, located on the Main, was for centuries an independent city-state and is today the chief financial city of Germany. The picturesque and famous German university town of Heidelberg is located on the Necker, where the South German Hills give way to the Black Forest.

The Black Forest, or Schwarzwald, is a thickly forested, mountainous region in southwestern Germany. Its dark forests of fir and spruce formed the scene for many German legends and fairy tales. The area's health resorts, such as Baden-Baden, are noted for their mineral springs. The people of the Black Forest have retained many of their local traditions and are still famous for the toys, cuckoo clocks, and musical instruments manufactured there.

The Alps, the largest system of mountains in Europe, rise in southern Bavaria (Bayern). The highest spot in Germany, the Zugspitze, rising 9,721 feet (2,963 meters) above sea level, is one of the many snow-capped mountains that make this region a vacation spot all year long. Munich (München), the principal city of Bavaria, lies north of the mountains in gently rolling land. It is famous for its museums, especially the German Technical Museum, its beer halls, such as the Hofbräu Haus, and its brass bands. It is the site of a gigantic Oktoberfest every autumn. Bavarian men sometimes wear their traditional costumes: Lederhosen (short leather pants with suspenders) and Tyrolean feathered caps. The traditional costume for women is the dirndl, the Alpine peasant dress with a full skirt, gathered bodice, and apron.

THE PEOPLE

Germany, which sent so many immigrants to America, was not only a complex place with a varied geography, with different political traditions, and with different local traditions and attitudes; its people were also quite diverse temperamentally, religiously, and economically.

The Germans who came to America from Bavaria, for example, dressed, talked, and acted quite differently from Germans in the north, who tended to be a bit more serious—or, as the southern Germans would say, more rigid—than the Catholic Bavarians and Rhinelanders. The Bavarians love shared good times and geniality, which they call *Gemütlichkeit*. They enjoyed listening to music in their beer halls and beer gardens. The music of Bavarian brass bands is what many Americans think of as "ump-pah-pah," or "German music." Like other Germans, the Bavarians tend to be hardworking and serious when those characteristics are called for, but they also love holiday fun, a trait they share with their fellow Catholic Germans along the Rhine River. In Rhineland cities such as Cologne, which was founded by Romans, the people celebrate the pre-Lenten carnival, which they call Fasching. This celebration, in a muted form, was brought to the United States.

In religious belief, a bit more than half of the population of the German Empire in 1871 were Protestants, and most of those Protestants were Lutherans or Calvinists. However, more than 40 percent of the population was Catholic, and there was a large Jewish community as well. The Germans who came to the United States and Canada were the most diverse of the major immigrant groups in both religion and occupation. They entered America at most of the major ports, and they spread throughout the United States and Canada.

Before 1871, most Germans were farmers. Though today Germany is an industrial country, its farmers are still noted for their hard work and their efforts to keep their farms neat and attractive. Neatly mowed pastures, clean fields surrounded by stone walls or hedges, clean barns, and sturdy, well-kept houses typify the German countryside. These characteristics of hard work and orderliness were brought to America by many of the German peasants, who came in search of cheap land. In Germany, farmers and peasants tended to live in agricultural towns and villages rather than on isolated farms. Town and city life were very important to Germans, who had a special attachment to their local community. Distances in America were so great and so much land was available that Germans often had to set up isolated farmsteads, but they still relished community life. Churches and villages became the center of German rural life in America.

The Federal Republic of Germany at play: a folk festival in Munich, 1989.

Germany had a long tradition of craftsmanship. Craftsmen were respected, and hard work was not looked down upon. In the towns and cities of Germany, craftsmen formed both economic and social organizations. German craftsmen organized guilds, which were forerunners of trade unions. With the coming of the Industrial Revolution in the nineteenth century, some of the old crafts were threatened by the developing factories and their automated methods of production.

In addition to their unions, craftsmen and workers had their social clubs and sports clubs. There is a saying that whenever three Germans get together they form a club. This is certainly an exaggeration, but Germans are attracted by small groups of people who share their interests and give them a sense of belonging. German workers brought to America not only pride in hard work and craftsmanship but also pride in themselves and their communities.

There is much that is admirable in the German character and in German traditions. The United States and Canada were enriched by the contributions of German immigrants to their societies and cultures.

WHY AMERICA?

German immigrants were the most diverse in background of all major immigrant groups, and they settled throughout the country. The availability of land and the desire for religious freedom drew the first Germans to America. Germans came to Virginia shortly after the founding of Jamestown, and early German settlers in Maryland gave their names to Port Herman and Hack's Point. Germans were also among the settlers who went to the Dutch colony of New Amsterdam, today New York, and New Sweden, today in the states of Delaware and New Jersey. Later they would help settle the Canadian and American frontier lands.

FREEDOM IN THE NEW WORLD

In 1683, a group of Mennonites led by Francis Pastorius left Krefeld in the Rhineland and sailed to Pennsylvania. William Penn, a Quaker, had organized his colony as a haven for the oppressed, and he recruited Germans for his new land. There, Pastorius and his followers founded Germantown. They were the first of the Pennsylvania "Dutch," as these settlers were called because they spoke German, or *Deutsch*. The Krefeld settlers were followed by other religious dissenters. The Moravians, or members of the Church of the Brethren, founded Bethlehem, Pennsylvania. The Amish, who settled in Lancaster County, have preserved their simple and austere way of life until today. By 1766, one-third of the people in Pennsylvania were German.

Germans also settled in other colonies. The British recruited Germans from the Palatinate along the Rhine River to settle in

Although the year is 1990, the Amish of Lancaster County, Pennsylvania, still use the horse and buggy for transportation, preserving a simple way of life.

the Mohawk Valley of New York. One large group of German immigrants consisted of Lutherans, whom the Prince Archbishop of Salzburg expelled from his land because they were not Catholics. Today, Salzburg is in Austria, but in 1733 it was one of the many small German states. In 1733, a large group of these Salzburg Lutherans settled near Savannah in the colony of Georgia. Another group of Germans settled in Nova Scotia in 1750. In 1753, a group of two thousand immigrants from the German state of Hanover, which was ruled by the King of England, founded the town of Lunenburg, which became the center of shipbuilding in Canada's Maritime Provinces.

The French also attempted to populate their colony,

Louisiana, by recruiting settlers from Germany. By 1721, hundreds of Germans had settled an area along the Mississippi River north of New Orleans. Many inhabitants of this area have names that were originally German, but their ancestors were assimilated into the dominant Cajun French culture of the area. Bayou des Allemands (French for "Bayou of the Germans") is the center of this area, which is still called the "German Coast."

THE PRICE OF PASSAGE

Many Germans came to America in the colonial period as "redemptioners." They were unable to pay for their own transportation, so they agreed to *redeem* their fare after arriving in America by being auctioned off as indentured servants. Families were split up. The redemptioners agreed to work for up to seven years, without pay, for people who would reimburse their transportation costs. After seven years, they were free to move to the frontier and establish their own farmsteads. For children, the period of indenture could be much longer: They were separated from their parents and required to work as servants without pay until they were twenty-one. If a husband or wife died halfway across the ocean, the survivor had to pay or else serve out the indenture of the dead spouse. Even worse, if both parents of a child died, the child was responsible for paying or working out the entire family's fares.

Some captains and unscrupulous recruiters, called Newlanders, told passengers that they were being taken to Philadelphia. The ship then sailed to another port, where the dealers could auction off their passengers for more money. Relatives and friends often waited in vain at Philadelphia, ready to pay the fares of the immigrants, who never arrived.

THE TUG OF WAR: AMERICA'S REVOLUTION

Some Germans did not come to America by choice. The rulers of six small German states rented soldiers to the British during the Revolutionary War. Many of these men, known as Hessians, deserted to the American side during the war. More chose to stay after it ended. Many of the approximately six thousand who did stay were among the first to cross the mountains into the frontier country. General George Armstrong Custer, who led the Battle of the Little Bighorn, was a descendant of one of the Hessians who remained. Twelve hundred soldiers of the Brunswick Company, recruited in Germany by the British to defend Canada, settled in

Hessian soldiers fight honorably in the Battle of Bennington, August 16, 1777, during the American Revolutionary War.

Ontario and the Maritime Provinces after they were discharged.

During the American Revolution, many German Americans enthusiastically joined the struggle for American independence. The conservatism of some Germans, however, made them reluctant to support the revolution. Others were pacifists by religious conviction. Some of the German sectarians, though unable to fight, were willing to offer material support to the American cause. Others, however, regarded any involvement in the struggle as evil. Germans unwilling or unable to support the Revolutionary War were harassed, and many, out of political or religious belief, sought refuge in the Upper Canada area of Ontario. In Canada, Mennonites and other religious pacifists found not only land but freedom from military service as well.

The American Revolution and the disturbances and wars that followed the French Revolution of 1789 in Europe interrupted German emigration to America. After peace was restored to Europe in 1815, however, the flow of Germans resumed and eventually turned into a flood. German states removed restrictions on emigration, and social and economic conditions in nineteenth century Germany fostered emigration. American businesses, ship owners, and even states sent recruiters to hire skilled German workers or to persuade Germans to come to populate and farm the vast and potentially fertile land of America's developing Midwest.

ECONOMIC OPPORTUNITY

Most of the Germans who came to America in the early part of the nineteenth century did not do so for political reasons. Until the latter part of the nineteenth century, most were farmers or peasants who were discouraged by crop failures or by the increase in the German population, which brought with it higher land prices and rents. Land in Germany was scarce and expensive, and the owners of estates were adapting their land to commercial agriculture. They increasingly hired agricultural laborers as they were needed rather than renting or letting out land on shares (sharecropping). Fewer people, as a result, could acquire land or make an adequate living as farm laborers.

In 1831, the German poet Heinrich Heine met a group of heavily laden Germans walking along the highway toward the French port of Le Havre. He asked them why they were leaving Germany, and they answered that they could not stand it any longer. They were fleeing arrogant authorities, privileged nobles, and high taxes.

A PROMISED LAND?

In Germany, word came from earlier immigrants or from the recruiters of the opportunities to be found in America. Handbooks and newspapers promoted emigration to America by touting its advantages. The refrain of one popular German song rang out, "In America everything is great!" During this time, a few paupers came, when towns paid their passage to get rid of them. Most German immigrants, however—even peasants—had possessions or even some land which they could sell to purchase their passage and to finance the start of their new life in America. There was plenty of fertile land, and it was cheap.

In 1829, a German named Gottfried Duden, who had spent three years living on a farm in Missouri, published a report praising the new land, where food and property were cheap, nature was beautiful, and life was easy. This report enticed thousands of Duden's countrymen—including well-educated aristocrats, scholars, and clergy—to migrate. Some tried their hand at farming and were dubbed "Latin Farmers" because of their ability to recite the classics in Latin and Greek while tilling the soil. Most, however, ended up in the cities, where many worked as lawyers, educators, or journalists. It turned out that Duden's utopia was not a promised land after all, and Duden was called "the Lying Dog."

DREAMS OF UTOPIA

Germans did not give up the idea of a promised land, however. Some immigrants came as organized groups to establish religious or social utopias in America, such as Harmony, Pennsylvania, or Amana, Iowa. In Duden's Missouri, one German-American society attempted to concentrate the inflow of immigrants into a little Germany that could be considered for statehood.

In Texas, another society, called the Society for the Care of German Immigrants in Texas, or the Adelsverein, gave money to Germans to settle land in the area of San Antonio and Austin, Texas. The society went bankrupt and the plan fell apart, but thousands of Germans became Texans because of the Adelsverein. The German-American town of Fredericksburg stems from this settlement, and President Lyndon Johnson is thought to have had some ancestors among these German Americans.

In response to political oppression at home, a group of young German intellectuals formed the Giessen Society in the hope of promoting plans for a democratic German state. When this plan would not work out in Germany, they traveled to the United States, where they began plans to create a German state in Missouri, Texas, or Wisconsin. Although they never achieved their goal of establishing a separate Germany in America, one of their leaders, Friedrich Münch, became a Missouri state senator.

These schemes to create a New World Germany arose from frustration with oppression in Germany that eventually led to the revolutions of 1848. All across Europe, people rebelled against oppressive governments and wanted more democratic freedoms. Some Germans also wanted to remain separate from the people in America who were of Anglo-Saxon descent. German Americans feared losing their culture in the "melting pot," and they disliked the Puritans' austere approach to life— particularly their stifling attitude toward Sundays. Germans relished their one day of rest, and they did not like the Protestant rules that forced them to limit their public activities on that day. For some radical Germans, therefore, the answer became a separate Germany in North America. For most German Americans, however, assimilation just took place more slowly.

THE FORTY-EIGHTERS

After the failure of a movement for German national unity and freedom in the 1830's and the repression of the revolutions that swept Europe in 1848, many educated and cultured German political radicals sought refuge in America. These Germans became known as "Forty-eighters" because they had fought in these revolutions. Only a few thousand of these Germans settled in the United States, but they were highly educated and had liberal political viewpoints. Many of them, like their predecessors in Missouri, became known as "Latin Farmers," and they influenced the cultural life of the American frontier. They started discussion groups, produced plays, and were opposed to slavery. The most famous of these Germans was Carl Schurz, who would make his mark in American politics by becoming the first German American elected to the United States Senate.

RELIGIOUS REFUGE

Several groups among the mid-nineteenth century German immigrants saw America as a safe haven for religious expression. Ten thousand Jews came to the United States from Bavaria in 1839 to escape social and economic restrictions, and they were followed by Jews from other German states. Around 1840, a number of Lutherans came as a result of their opposition to the forced unification of the Lutheran and Reformed churches by the state of Prussia. In the 1870's, many Catholics, especially priests and nuns, left to escape Otto von Bismarck's anti-Catholic campaign, known as the *Kulturkampf*. Other Germans emigrated to avoid the compulsory military service, which had been established by Prussia in 1807 and then imposed upon all of Germany after it was united under Prussian leadership in 1871.

THE RUSSIAN GERMANS

Beginning in the 1870's, groups of Russian Germans began to arrive in the United States. They had originally been invited by Catherine the Great to settle along the Volga River near the Black Sea; she needed the Germans to farm the land. A century later, their population had grown so large that the Russians demanded that the Germans integrate with the local population and serve in the Russian army. These Catholic, Lutheran, Reformed, and Mennonite Germans—who felt strongly that they must maintain their separate ethnic and religious identities—began to leave for North America, settling in the American frontier states and Canada.

German-speaking Mennonites came to Canada to escape persecution in czarist Russia. Seven thousand of them settled on the prairies of Manitoba between 1874 and 1889. They would be followed in the 1920's by another community of German-speaking Mennonites, who sought refuge from the Russian Communists in the Fraser Valley of British Columbia.

A related group of Germany-speaking religious dissenters, the Hutterites, fled from Russia and settled in the Dakotas and Montana in 1874. They attempted to imitate the first Christians by practicing community ownership of property. Local intolerance for their Christian communalism led many to migrate to Canada in 1918. They set up communities called Bruderhofs, each of which had about one hundred members. Today there are approximately 130 Bruderhofs in South Dakota and Montana. Most, however, are located in the prairies of Canada, where some ten thousand Hutterites live today.

WAVES ACROSS THE FRONTIER

Most Germans, about two-thirds of the total, traveled to America not as utopians or political idealists or even religious refugees, but as family groups or individuals seeking a better way of life and economic opportunities. As Germany industrialized after 1848, many craftsmen—threatened by new technology, which made their skills obsolete—took advantage of the demand for skilled labor in America. German workers were highly regarded in their new home, and they were actively recruited. Many unskilled German workers, discouraged by the scarcity of jobs and depression at home and hearing of opportunity in America, also came in search of employment.

As steamships became more numerous, the voyage across the Atlantic became cheaper and quicker. Sailing vessels had taken as long as six weeks to travel from Germany to America. The trip was hard, and many of the early immigrants died on the way. Steamships now reduced the length of the voyage to two weeks. This encouraged greater immigration, but to leave home and go to a new land was still a difficult decision. Hardship was likely and disaster still possible. In 1858, when fire destroyed the immigrant ship *Austria*, 553 immigrants died and only 89 were saved. In the winter of 1867, typhoid fever aboard the Hamburg ship *Leibnitz* killed 108 of 544 passengers.

Nevertheless, Germans continued to emigrate in large numbers well through the end of the century. The presence and success of earlier immigrants led to chain migrations from German villages to specific places in America, with three major crests occurring in the years 1853-1855, 1866-1869, and the largest in 1881-1883.

The first wave was part of a larger migration, as German peasants and farmers fled the crop failures and starvation in the dwindling countryside for better opportunities elsewhere—either in the German cities or in the New World. Such opportunities were to be found. For example, it was right about this time that the California Gold Rush began: In 1847, a German American by the name of John Sutter discovered

A mass of emigrants board the Hamburg-Amerika Line—*the beginning of their journey to America.*

gold in a creek bed near his sawmill. Over the next several years, people from all over the world poured into California. As the population boomed, both established and new German Americans took advantage of the situation to start vineyards near San Francisco and to farm wheat in the Sacramento Valley.

The second wave of German immigrants reached America as the Civil War was ending and the unrest leading to Europe's Franco-Prussian War was beginning. During this period, the "push" of bad times at home was accompanied by the "pull" of American frontier. All over the New World, immigrants were needed to develop the land, contribute their skills, and provide services. Agencies and recruiters in America helped Germans immigrate and get settled. It was just before this period, in 1862, that the Homestead Act was passed in the United States. This law practically gave away land to anyone who would settle on it and help develop it, and many immigrants took advantage of this opportunity.

Finally, as population grew and the frontier started to fill up, America's Industrial Revolution expanded, and German workers and artisans were in even higher demand. The railroads and industries needed their skills. At the same time, many fellow Germans were already at home in the new land. Once German settlers had successfully established themselves in a town or in a part of the country, their presence became a sort of magnet attracting other Germans. Newcomers found it easier to adjust to conditions in America in the midst of fellow Germans who spoke their language and shared their culture, and the Homestead Act continued to be in effect until 1890.

A NEW WAVE: THE TWO WORLD WARS

The closing of the American frontier occurred as Germany's industrial development was gaining strength, and as Germany became more prosperous fewer Germans chose to leave their home country. Displaced or impoverished German farm workers increasingly sought jobs in German industrial cities, and emigration from Germany declined. Many Germans, however, continued to come until 1914, when World War I cut Germany off from the United States.

After that war ended in 1918, economic distress in defeated Germany led to a new wave of German immigrants. This new surge was tempered when, in 1924, the U.S. government passed laws to restrict the number of immigrants entering the United States.

After Adolf Hitler came to power in 1933, another group of German immigrants sought safety and freedom in America. Hitler's Nazi regime, intolerant of opposition, persecuted anyone who challenged its ideas and especially anyone who did not fit its racist categories. As a result, Nazis harassed and eventually attempted to exterminate "undesirables" such as the Jewish people. Jews and other victims of Nazi oppression sought refuge in the United States. However, because of more immigration quotas imposed by the U.S. government in 1928, only a portion of those who wanted to come to America were allowed entry. By the end of World War II, 140,000 German Jews had come to the United States.

In the 1930's, the United States was suffering from the Great Depression, and many people were unemployed. In addition to the overcoming quota restrictions, prospective immigrants had to demonstrate that they could support themselves. Among the Germans who were allowed to settle in the United States were prominent German educators, scientists, writers, and musicians. The new German Americans included the great physicist Albert Einstein, the Nobel Prize-winning novelist Thomas Mann, the psychologist Bruno Bettelheim, the theologian Paul Tillich, the conductor Bruno Walter, and the architects Walter Gropius and Ludwig Mies van der Rohe.

After the war, Germany was a devastated and occupied land. The Russians had established themselves in the eastern part of Germany and organized a puppet Communist regime there. Millions of German-speaking people had fled the advance of the Red Army or had been expelled from their homes in Poland, Czechoslovakia, and elsewhere in Eastern Europe by people resentful of the aggression and atrocities of Nazi Germany. Among the refugees allowed to enter the United States after the war were additional German Jews and displaced German-speaking people seeking security, freedom, and opportunity.

Prosperity was eventually restored in the Federal Republic of Germany, or West Germany, through hard work and foreign aid from the United States. Prosperity and opportunity in Germany drastically decreased the number of Germans who were interested in permanently emigrating to America. Some Germans, however—inspired by a sense of adventure and a desire to take advantage of their special talents—continued to emigrate. When, on October 3, 1990, the two Germanies were reunited, an entire generation of East Germans—who had grown up under a totalitarian government—suddenly faced the new freedoms, and new responsibilities, of a democratic state. Many political observers wondered what effect, if any, their new political freedoms would have on their lives, attitudes, and choices.

WHEN THEY CAME

One of the first Europeans to come to America was a German. According to Icelandic sagas, "Tyrker the German" was a crew member with the Viking explorer Leif Ericson. When the Vikings landed along the coast of present-day New England, around A.D. 1000, Tyrker is supposed to have found grapes. Leif then called the area Vineland.

Estimates for the total number of German-speaking people who came to North America during the colonial period vary widely. Some historians place the figure as low as 65,000. Some, on the other hand, estimate that as many as 100,000 German-speaking people settled in the region of the thirteen original states before 1776.

THE UNITED STATES

In the period since the American Revolution, more Germans have come to the United States than any other national group. From 1815 to 1914, 5.5 million Germans came to the United States. Since World War I, 1.5 million have come. This amounts to almost 15 percent of the total number of immigrants who came to the United States. During much of the second half of the 1800's and between 1923 and 1963, more Germans immigrated than members of any other national group. In every decade between 1830 and 1890, Germans constituted at least a quarter of all immigrants to America, and in the 1850's and the 1860's, Germans constituted more than one-third of the new arrivals.

The peak years of German immigration were 1854 and 1882. In 1854, 215,000 arrived, and 250,000 settled in the new land in 1882. Approximately 90 percent of all the people leaving Germany between 1835 and 1910 came to the United States.

World Wars I and II interrupted the immigration of Germans to America. After World War I, there was a renewed surge of immigration prompted by bad economic conditions in Germany. Then immigration restrictions limited access to the United States during the 1930's. After World War II, there was another surge, as German-speaking people fleeing chaos in Germany and Eastern Europe were allowed to enter the United States in large numbers.

Following the war, Germany was divided into zones of occupation controlled by the United States, Great Britain, France, and the Soviet Union. Approximately ten million Germans—fleeing the Russians or expelled from their homes by resentful Eastern Europeans—crowded into the western zones of occupation and were amalgamated. In 1949, they became the Federal Republic of Germany, or West Germany. The Russians responded by organizing their satellite domain into the German Democratic Republic, or East Germany. Thousands of Germans fled the repressive regime of East Germany for the freedom and prosperity of West Germany. To prevent the loss of so many of its young and talented people, the Communist regime erected the Berlin Wall in 1961. This monstrosity reinforced and symbolized the division of Germany. It came between family members and neighbors, just as Germans had been separated from one another within their own country.

Despite the trauma of division, self-confidence had been restored in democratic West Germany by the 1960's, and the country reached previously unattained levels of prosperity. The standard of living in Germany was so high and opportunity so great that after 1962 the number of German immigrants to the United States never reached the quota level assigned to

Germany, and many Germans who came to America returned to Germany after a few years. Even so, Germany shares with Italy, Portugal, and Great Britain, among the European countries, the record of having sent more than 10,000 immigrants to the United States in a single year since 1964, and 200,000 Germans immigrated to the United States between 1961 and 1970. The numbers declined to 66,000 for the period from 1971 to 1980.

Between 1961 and 1985, 300,500 Germans immigrated to the United States, exceeded only by 587,900 Chinese (from China, Taiwan, and Hong Kong), 354,600 Italians, and 327,700 Indians, who came during the same period.

CANADA

By 1931, 473,544 Canadians were of German descent. A wave of German immigration to Canada had occurred from 1880 to 1914. The number of German inhabitants in Saskatchewan rocketed from 5,000 in 1901 to 100,000 in 1911. By the outbreak of World War I, there were 35,000 Germans in Manitoba. The war, however, ended the favorable treatment of Germans wishing to enter Canada. In the 1920's, German-speaking immigrants had to agree to work on farms for a few years to gain permission to enter the country.

The Great Depression and World War II practically cut off immigration to Canada. Faced with its own economic crisis, Canada refused to allow entry to the many German Jews who sought to escape Hitler's regime. German Canadians received better treatment during World War II than they had in World War I. During the early war years, 6,700 Germans and Austrians were deported to Canada from Britain. When they were released from detention in 1943, 5,200 chose to stay in Canada.

In the 1950's, approximately a quarter of a million Germans, many of them ethnic Germans, or *Volksdeutsche*,

German Immigration to the United States: 1820-1985

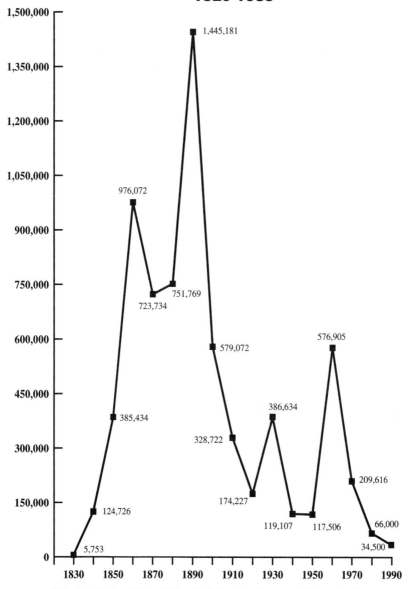

Note: Statistics from 1820 to 1871 are limited to those German-speaking people who came to the United States from the territories that were united in 1871 to form the German Empire. After 1871, the statistics include only those German-speaking immigrants who lived in the German state.

from Eastern European countries, immigrated to Canada. New immigration regulations were established in 1958 to decrease all immigration, but since the 1970's an increasing number of German business people have been welcomed.

WHERE THEY LIVE

Until 1830, the immigrants who arrived in America from Germany had settled mainly New York, New Jersey, Pennsylvania, Maryland, and Virginia. From there, they had worked their way into Ohio and other parts of the Midwest. This area became known as the "German Triangle." Outside this area, Germans could also be found in New Orleans, Louisiana; St. Louis, Missouri; rural areas of Texas; and San Francisco, California. After 1830, accelerated immigration spread these settlers across wider areas of the country.

THE EASTERN CONCENTRATION

Until the redemptioner trade was ended by American legislation in 1819, most German immigrants arrived on Dutch ships at ports on the Atlantic coast of America, especially Baltimore, New York, Philadelphia, and Charleston. In the colonial period and in the first decades of the United States' existence, Pennsylvania had the greatest concentration of German inhabitants. One-third of its population was German. There were significant numbers of Germans in Maryland, New Jersey, and New York. Some Germans had also settled in South Carolina and Georgia and along the frontier.

THE SOUTH: RETURN "CARGO"

After 1819, German immigrants provided return cargo for ships that brought cotton to Le Havre, in France, and tobacco to Bremen, in Germany. Between 1820 and 1850, the cotton boats brought 53,909 Germans to New Orleans. During the next ten years, the number climbed to 200,000. Thousands stayed there and contributed to the growth and development of that city. The majority, however, took boats up the Mississippi River and settled in the Missouri, Ohio, and Mississippi river valleys. The tobacco ships brought Germans to Baltimore, where they augmented the old German community or from where they moved to the Ohio river valley and beyond.

German farmers eventually tended to avoid the South because of the climate, the lack of good land at cheap prices, and the competition of slave labor or, after the Civil War, of underpaid African-American workers. A number of German Jews, however—attracted by opportunities in the market and railroad towns of the South—established successful stores and businesses there. Mexico and the Republic of Texas were able to attract a number of Germans to Texas before it became a part of the United States, by promising freedom from taxes. Other Germans, encouraged by the success of the first settlers, followed. New Braunfels and Fredericksburg in the Brazos Valley became the center of a large German community. There were approximately 60,000 Germans in the South at the time of the Civil War, and nearly 20,000 of them lived in New Orleans.

THE EXPANSION WEST

In Germany, Hamburg eventually became the greatest port of departure for German emigrants, and the North German Lloyd and Hamburg-American ship companies transported Germans from Hamburg to New York. Many Germans, attracted by the vitality of New York and the opportunity for industrial labor in Hoboken and Newark, New Jersey, did not move any farther. Some immigrants were stranded by their poverty in the port cities of the East. Many German immigrants, however, had sufficient resources to move farther west. They were drawn by cheap land and established farms first in the Midwest and then on the Great Plains.

Germans gather in a "Migrant Village" near Hamburg, before departing for America. Many became stranded in villages such as this.

The German immigrants went up the Hudson River and along the Erie Canal to the Great Lakes and the Midwest. After 1850, Wisconsin and other states actively recruited German immigrants both at German ports and after they had arrived in America. Northern Pacific Railroad agents also persuaded Germans to settle along their line to populate and develop the Northern Great Plains and to increase the railroad's business.

By the twentieth century, the preferred areas of German settlement extended along a "German Belt" from New York through Pennsylvania, Ohio, Indiana, and Illinois. Branches of the German Belt spread into Michigan, Wisconsin, Minnesota, Iowa, Missouri, Kansas, and Nebraska. Other areas of significant German settlement were Louisiana, Texas, Colorado, Utah, California, Oregon, Washington, and Montana. According to the U.S. census of 1910, 522,252 Germans farmers constituted the largest ethnic group among American farmers.

"LITTLE GERMANY": THE URBAN DWELLERS

Approximately 70 percent of German Americans lived in cities and towns. By the year 1900, 36 percent of the German-born population resided in only fifteen cities. This concentration allowed the Germans to build strong communities with many shared activities. They dominated entire neighborhoods, and many cities had "Little Germanies" consisting of German-style houses, and German-speaking shops, churches, and social life.

German workers and business people settled in the growing cities of America's Midwest. St. Louis, Louisville, and Cincinnati attracted many German immigrants before the Civil War. In 1860, there were 50,000 German-born people in St. Louis and nearly 44,000 in Cincinnati. Later immigrants increasingly chose Milwaukee, Chicago, Detroit, Cleveland, and Toledo. Minneapolis and Milwaukee had particularly large numbers of German inhabitants.

The Germans contributed a marked and enduring character to Milwaukee, where the German-born population grew from 15,981 in 1860 to 68,969 in 1900. In the middle of the nineteenth century, half of the city's inhabitants were Germans. Many lived in their own section, Germantown, where they re-created a German community in the middle of the United

States. Their houses looked like German houses; their signs were in German; they spoke German; and they acted like Germans.

Some Germans even advocated the establishment of their own state, "New Germany," in Wisconsin. It never came to that, but their imprint is still evident. Most German Americans agreed with Carl Schurz, who said, "We as Germans are not called upon here to form a separate nationality but rather to contribute to the American nationality the strongest there is in us, and in place of our weakness to substitute the strength wherein our fellow Americans excel us."

Schurz's vision prevailed. Today Germans have spread throughout America and American society. Few of the old German neighborhoods remain. Germans have moved and have been replaced by others. Scotch-Irish people from Appalachia now dominate Cincinnati's old Over-the-Rhine neighborhood. Milwaukee's North Side and Germantown, Pennsylvania, are predominantly African American.

CANADA

Many of the nineteenth and early twentieth century German-speaking immigrants to Canada were members of religious groups seeking the freedom to follow their special way of life without persecution. They settled on the plains of Manitoba and Saskatchewan and in the Fraser Valley of British Columbia. Catholic and Lutheran Germans were also drawn by the availability of productive farmland in Canada. Non-Mennonite Germans settled around Winnipeg in Manitoba, Regina in Saskatchewan, and Edmonton in Alberta.

In the middle of the nineteenth century, a number of German Jews settled in Toronto, Montreal, Vancouver, and Hamilton. After World War I, many skilled workers and technicians emigrated from Germany to the cities of English-speaking Canada. In the 1950's another large wave of skilled

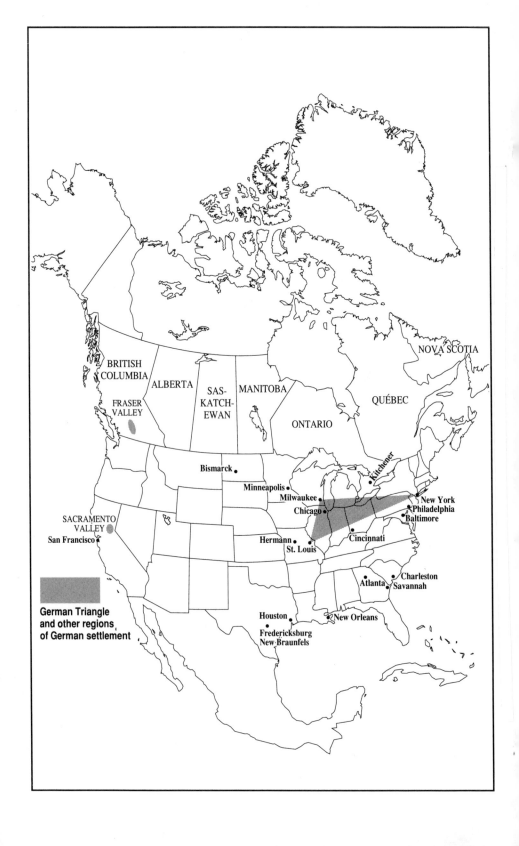

BRITISH
COLUMBIA

ALBERTA

SAS-
KATCH-
EWAN

MANITOBA

ONTARIO

QUÉBEC

NOVA SCOTIA

FRASER
VALLEY

Bismarck

Minneapolis

Milwaukee

Chicago

Kitchener

New York
Philadelphia
Baltimore

SACRAMENTO
VALLEY

San Francisco

Hermann

St. Louis

Cincinnati

Charleston
Savannah

Atlanta

Houston

New Orleans

Fredericksburg
New Braunfels

German Triangle
and other regions
of German settlement

and educated German immigrants settled in cities such as Toronto and Vancouver.

WHERE ARE THEY TODAY?

Germans were different from many other immigrant groups in the nineteenth century, because they dispersed across the country. As a result, Germans today are more equally distributed throughout the territory of the United States than any other ethnic group.

Today the largest number of people of German descent in Canada, more than 370,000, live in the province of Ontario. There are 233,175 living in Alberta; 187,630 in British Columbia; 161,700 in Saskatchewan; 108,140 in Manitoba; and 33,145 in Nova Scotia. Only 33,770 reside in the large, French-speaking province of Quebec.

In the United States, New York has always had more German-born citizens than any other state. It contained 18 percent of the German-born Americans in 1880 and 22 percent in 1970.

Since the second half of the nineteenth century, however, Wisconsin has had the highest percentage of Germans in its population. Particularly when second- and third-generation German Americans are counted, Wisconsin and Minnesota are the most "German" of all states in the nation. Other states with particularly high percentages of native Germans have been Illinois, Ohio, and Pennsylvania.

Since the 1960's, new centers of Germans have emerged, including Houston, Texas, and Atlanta, Georgia, where German industry has established branches. By 1970, California and New Jersey had displaced Illinois and Pennsylvania as the second and fourth favorite choices of residence by people who were coming directly from Germany.

German "Old Town Village" in Garden Grove, California—keeping the heritage alive in the 1990's.

WHAT THEY DO

In 1870, 37 percent of the working Germans in the United States were skilled workers; 27 percent were farmers; 23 percent were professionals, such as musicians, artists, or teachers; and 13 percent were involved in business or transportation. This profile largely mirrored the work experience of these Germans before they emigrated. In 1875, one-third of the German immigrants who listed an occupation stated that they were skilled workers. One-fourth said that they were farmers, and another fourth said that they were unskilled workers. The number of farmers and skilled workers among the new arrivals subsequently declined.

SKILLED AND UNSKILLED WORKERS

Industrial development in Germany created demand for skilled workers, and as the American frontier closed, workers from the German countryside often sought their fortunes in the growing cities of industrial Germany. In 1890, 45 percent of German American immigrants stated that they were unskilled workers, but as the new factories of Germany acquired enough skilled workers, skilled and semiskilled workers again turned to America for new opportunities.

German artisans or skilled workers were valued because of their skills and industriousness. It was not uncommon in later nineteenth century America to see industries advertising for German workers. Unskilled German immigrants tended to move to the Midwestern cities to avoid the competing concentration of unskilled Irish workers on the East Coast. In the Midwest, competition for menial jobs was not quite as intense, and the Germans' reputation for industriousness was an advantage. Unskilled German workers in the 1850's constituted more than a third of the work force in St. Louis and Detroit.

FARMERS

Many German farmers were attracted to the United States and Canada by cheap or even free land. They played a central role in developing the agriculture of the Midwest and the Great Plains. In 1870, one-third of the foreign-born farmers in the United States were German, and by 1900, German Americans owned 11 percent of the country's farms. Today, more American farmers trace their heritage to Germany than to any other country.

German farmers were very conservative and relied on family labor to work their land. They avoided debt and viewed their farms as a family legacy rather than as disposable property. Their sense of permanence and their industriousness led them to erect substantial and attractive farm buildings and to nurture and conserve the land. These characteristics can still be observed on the German-American farms and dairies of the Midwest and Great Plains.

THE FAMILY ENTERPRISE

At times an entire family worked in the family business, such as a retail store, bakery, or tailor shop. Businesses were often run by groups of relatives. Sons worked with fathers, learning the trade so they would be prepared to take over the business when the father could no longer run it.

Germans who established businesses usually hired other Germans. This made it possible for new immigrants to settle in neighborhoods near earlier immigrants. In the late nineteenth century, newcomers stayed at boardinghouses or cheap hotels. Many also stayed with friends and relatives or

Two German Americans take a lunch break from their work in a machine shop. The 1940's in Frankenmuth, Michigan.

boarded with German families. Most families across the social classes had relatives or boarders living with them. This provided an additional source of household income.

BECOMING ESTABLISHED

There was a tendency for second- and third-generation urban German Americans to become white-collar workers or even professionals such as doctors and lawyers. Professionals were particularly numerous among German immigrants after World War I. The economic, educational, and social advancement of German Americans, however, was near the national norm.

In 1972, the median income of German Americans was above the national norm, but their schooling and their advancement into the professions and management occurred at a somewhat lower rate than the average for second-generation Americans of all nationalities. The median family income for German Americans in 1972 was below that of Russian, Polish, Italian, British, and Irish Americans.

BUTCHERS, BAKERS, BEER MAKERS

Germans became involved in all sorts of retail trade. There were German bakers and butchers. Some Germans opened grocery stores, others restaurants, bars, and beer halls. Germans established breweries, and German workers made the beer. Germans practiced the traditional skills of carpentry, cabinetmaking, tailoring, shoemaking, plumbing, tanning, printing, blacksmithing, brick making, and carriage and wagon making. Germans opened horticultural nurseries and specialized in dairy farming. Some Germans practiced the tedious and low-paying skill of cigar making.

Among these skilled jobs, perhaps the one that is most "German" is that of the brewer, or beer maker: Germans brought to America a taste for their national drink, beer. Other Germans, often people who had worked in breweries in Germany, founded breweries in the United States and Canada. In Germany, the contents of beer and the brewing process are strictly regulated. Apart from specific exceptions granted to a single brewery, all German beer is made from malted barley and hops. In the United States and Canada, beer is sometimes made from malted rice and corn.

THE MILITARY

The military was regarded as a most honored profession in the state of Prussia during the nineteenth century, and it was Prussia that used its military prowess to unite Germany.

Frederick the Great and General Helmut von Moltke stand out in the history of military theory and leadership as important figures.

Many German Americans have exhibited the same discipline, sense of honor, and skill that characterized the military profession in Germany. The head of the U.S. forces in Europe during World War I, General John Pershing, was from a German-American family originally named Pförschin. Dwight David Eisenhower, the thirty-fourth president of the United States, served during World War II as commander of the Allied forces; he also had German ancestors. In the Gulf War of 1991, the commanding general was another German American, General Norman Schwarzkopf.

BUSINESS: THE ENTREPRENEURIAL SPIRIT

Though the story of most Germans in America is not one of a dramatic rise from poverty to riches, some German immigrants had exceptional success. It is perhaps characteristic that a number of the success stories are related to the manufacture of clothing, food items, and musical instruments. John Jacob Astor was twenty years old when he arrived in New York in 1784. At the time of his death in 1848, he was the richest man in America. He had become a millionaire through the fur trade. Levi Strauss, who came to America in 1843, headed to California after gold was discovered there in 1848. His fortune was made when the pants fashioned out of covered-wagon canvas led to the manufacture of Levi "jeans." Henry Steinway became a prominent manufacturer of pianos, and Frederick Weyerhäuser a wealthy lumberman. The Busch, Pabst, Schaefer, and Schlitz families became successful brewers of beer, the national German drink.

CONTRIBUTIONS TO

SOCIETY

Though Germans did not found the colonies in North America or form the bulk of their population, they were present from the early days of settlement. They not only contributed to the physical growth of America but also had an impact on the formation of U.S. and Canadian culture. Many things which are today considered to be uniquely American have their roots in the industrious and convivial German immigrants.

NAMING A NATION

German map makers gave the name "America" to the land discovered by Christopher Columbus. In 1507, Martin Waldseemüller suggested that the New World be named after Americus (Amerigo) Vespucci, an Italian explorer, who had reached the coast of South America in 1497. Gerhard Kremer, who changed his name to the Latin version, Gerard Mercator, solidified the use of the name in his famous atlas published in the Rhenish town of Duisburg in 1594.

ESTABLISHING A STATE

The first governor of the Dutch colony, New Netherlands, was Peter Minuit or Minnewit, a German from Wesel in the Rhineland. In 1626, Minuit traded with the local Indians, giving them goods that were worth approximately twenty-four dollars in exchange for Manhattan Island. On this island he laid the foundation for the largest city of the United States. The name of the colony and the town, New Amsterdam, was changed to New York after the British seized control of the area in 1664.

BUILDING A DEMOCRACY

Jacob Leisler, who had been born in Frankfurt, was governor of the British colony from 1689 to 1691. He championed the interests of the common people against the wealthy landowners and merchants. Their resentment led to his replacement and prosecution. A kangaroo court consisting of his chief opponents found him guilty of treason and, with his son-in-law, he was hanged on May 16, 1691. He is regarded as an early martyr to justice and self-government.

Another early German New Yorker, John Peter Zenger, was a champion of freedom in colonial America. He criticized the English governor in his newspaper and in 1734 was accused of libel. The government thought that it could easily suppress this nuisance, but Zenger's attorney made an issue of the government's abuses. The jury's acquittal of Zenger marked a significant step toward freedom of the press in America.

Some Germans refused to support the American Revolution out of loyalty to the English government or, as was more often the case, because of religiously inspired pacifism. Many, however, not only supported the Revolution but fought and died for it, too. A force of New York Germans commanded by Nikolas Herkimer prevented the British General Saint Leger from joining General Burgoyne. This contributed to the American victory at Saratoga, which was a turning point in the war.

TOOLS FOR THE PIONEERS

German craftsmen gave America some essential tools of its frontier period. The covered wagons of America's western expansion were modified versions of the Conestoga wagon designed and built by the Germans of Pennsylvania. Pennsylvania Germans also designed and manufactured the accurate and relatively light rifles called Kentucky long rifles. These rifles were used by frontiersmen like Daniel Boone and Davy Crocket, and by General Andrew Jackson's troops from Kentucky and Tennessee at the Battle of New Orleans in 1815.

Smithsonian Institution

The finely crafted Kentucky rifle was state-of-the-art in the Old West.

German immigrants in the nineteenth century helped to transform the frontier into productive farms. They helped to built our cities. They worked in factories and constructed the railroads that moved people and produce west. As early as 1819, John Quincy Adams, then the U.S. secretary of state, wrote:

> Neither the general government of the Union, nor those of the individual states, are ignorant or unobservant of the additional strength and wealth, which accrues to the nation, by the accession of a mass of healthy, industrious, and frugal laborers, nor are they in any manner insensible to the great benefits which this country has derived and continues to derive, from the influx of such adoptive children from Germany.

Known for their precision clockwork, the Germans are famous for their ornate cuckoo clocks.

David Fowler

SHAPING A CULTURE

Germans not only helped to build America materially; they also contributed to a broadening of American culture. Along with other immigrants, they helped to humanize the harsh Puritanism of some of the early colonists. The Germans opposed the Blue Laws, which restricted activities on Sundays. Though most Germans were churchgoers, they also saw Sunday as an opportunity for recreation. They enjoyed visiting one another and going to parks or on picnics. They also took advantage of the day off to organize concerts, theatricals, and dances. They established and patronized beer gardens, where they gathered to enjoy congenial talk and music, and they often spent Sunday afternoons there.

Some Americans objected to the outlook of the Germans and their behavior. The Know-Nothings, those Americans who believed that "their" America was threatened by the influx of foreigners (especially Catholics), attacked Irish and German immigrants and burned their churches. In the German section of Louisville, Kentucky, anti-foreign rioters killed twenty German Americans in 1855. In this pre-Civil War climate, German Americans were attacked for their liberal politics, their opposition to slavery, and their fondness for beer-drinking and Sunday recreation at a time when the religiously inspired temperance movement and Blue Laws were widespread. German Americans withstood these attacks and went on to make their mark on the national psyche.

HOLIDAY TRADITIONS

Germans were responsible for the development of Christmas into the most important American holiday. Before the great influx of German immigrants in the nineteenth century, not all Americans observed the holiday. The Germans not only introduced the Christmas tree to America but also brought with them their fondness for this family-oriented time. Though the contemporary holiday has been commercialized and expanded into a whole "holiday season," it has its roots in the cutting and decorating of spruce trees by early German Americans.

Even the classic North American image of Santa Claus was provided by a German. Thomas Nast, the famous nineteenth century political cartoonist, was an immigrant from the Palatinate on the Rhine River. His drawing of a fat, jolly, and bearded Santa Claus was printed on the cover of *Harper's Weekly*. To this day, Nast's version of "Pelznikel," the St. Nicholas of Palatine folklore, remains familiar and is reprinted many times each Christmas season.

The Germans began their Christmas celebration two weeks before Christmas day. "Knecht Ruprecht" (another name for Santa Claus) came with his rod to bring apples, nuts, and candy to good children and to threaten bad children. On Christmas Eve, the Christmas tree was decorated with candles, candy, cookies, and fruit. The entire family then gathered around the tree. They sang songs, read the Bible, and gave one another presents. The activities on Christmas Day and the day after Christmas centered on the family, church, and friends.

The Germans also celebrated Sylvester Abend, New Year's Eve, at home and at club gatherings. They enjoyed dancing, playing cards, eating and drinking, and exchanging New Year's wishes. A unique custom which the Germans brought to America was shooting in the New Year. A group of men called shooters went from house to house singing, playing musical instruments, making New Year wishes, and making noise by shooting guns to welcome in the New Year. (This practice, which is illegal in many crowded urban areas today, was probably less dangerous in the less populated times when it was introduced to America.)

Thomas Nast's famous illustration of Santa Claus for the cover of Harper's Weekly.

A HERITAGE OF IMAGINATION

German folklore, through the stories of the Brothers Jacob and Wilhelm Grimm, became part of the legacy of all Americans. Schneewittchen has become Snow White; Dornröschen, Sleeping Beauty; and Rotkäppchen, Little Red Riding Hood. Rumpelstilzchen needs little translation to become Rumpelstiltskin, and there are Hansel and Gretel and many more.

Germans established theaters and operas, and their love for music had a lasting impact upon America. They were responsible for the establishment of many of the symphony orchestras, such as the New York Philharmonic Orchestra, which was initially called the Germania Orchestra. They also founded many choral societies and glee clubs.

EDUCATION FOR YOUNG AND OLD

One of the most significant and far-reaching of German contributions to American life was the preschool for young children, or the *Kindergarten* ("children's garden"). Kindergartens were started in Germany by Friedrich Fröbel and introduced to the United States by Margaretha Meyer Schurz (the wife of Carl Schurz), who established the first American kindergarten in Watertown, Wisconsin, in 1855. In 1873, W. T. Harris, the superintendent for public schools in St. Louis, made the kindergarten part of the public school system there.

Germans promoted higher education by establishing free state universities, which would provide training in scientific and technical skills as well as the humanities at low prices. Such institutions were common in Germany. Michigan was the first state to establish such a system, and it was followed by Wisconsin. The Johns Hopkins University was patterned on German universities. Students had to possess an undergraduate degree to be admitted. The German practice of research was stressed. This set the pattern for graduate programs in America.

HEALTHY MIND, HEALTHY BODY

Germans founded athletic clubs known as *Turnvereine*. These German fraternal organizations, begun in Germany in the early 1800's by Friedrich Jahn, were intended to foster German patriotism and nationalism. In the new land, they served to instill traditional values of physical excellence in German American youth. *Turnvereine* mushroomed in German-American communities when they were introduced in the mid-1800's, and sometimes they were used to propagate political viewpoints—especially against the Know-Nothings.

The legacy of the *Turnvereine*, however, is that they fostered physical fitness and sports, and in many ways they were the source of the gymnasiums and spas now familiar as school and community facilities. Some see in the German emphasis on physical education the root of present-day physical education classes and school teams. The notion of athletic clubs, which would promote character training as well as physical exercise, was also incorporated into the YMCA and YWCA organizations.

DEFENDING THE DOWNTRODDEN

Many German immigrants in the first half of the nineteenth century joined the Democratic Party, which supported immigrants against the bias of the prejudiced. Some Germans, however, helped to found the Republican Party in 1854, and many other Germans rallied to the new party. Having come to the United States in search of democratic rights and the freedom to make their own future, German Americans were opposed to the extension of slavery into new territories, and many advocated the abolition of that inhumane institution. The first recorded protest against the enslavement of African

Americans in America had been made by German settlers in Germantown, Pennsylvania, in 1688.

The Germans who followed those early settlers rallied to the union cause in the Civil War. Charles Sumner, an abolitionist and Senator from Massachusetts, said that without the support of German Americans, Abraham Lincoln would not have been elected President. A greater percentage of German Americans served in the union army than did native-born Americans. In all, about 180,000 young German Americans wore the Union blue. Seventeen German Americans became generals, and many others were officers. German-American militia units saved St. Louis and then Missouri for the Union.

On August 14, 1864, barely one thousand men of the all-German Second Missouri Infantry defended Dalton, Georgia, on the Chattanooga & Atlanta Railroad against six thousand Confederate cavalry troops. The Confederate commander, General Joseph Wheeler, several times demanded that the German-born colonel, Bernhard Laiboldt, surrender. His response was, "I have been placed here to hold this post, not surrender it. Come and get me!"

Following the Civil War, the number of German immigrants increased as economic depression made life in Germany more difficult for working people. Unions of workers and the involvement of workers in politics were prominent developments in Germany after 1870, and German workers brought those notions with them to their new country. Hoping to find greater opportunity and freedom here, many German working people played a significant role in the development of the American trade union movement.

OVERCOMING WARTIME PREJUDICE

There was a wave of anti-German feeling during World War I. Narrow-minded people, who believed that they were being patriotic, thought of German Americans as "Huns." They changed German-derived street names and even removed the books of famous German authors from libraries. Sauerkraut was called "liberty cabbage"; the hamburger became the "Salisbury steak"; and dachshunds were transformed into patriotic little "liberty hounds." The nationalist furor even led to attacks on German Americans. Descendants of Germans, however, served their country in that war—as they had in others—as loyally as had people of other national backgrounds. The most famous American air ace in World War I was Eddie Richenbacher.

Fifteen years later, at the brink of World War II, Adolf Hitler found few supporters among the Germans of America. German Americans were proud of their heritage but they were also completely loyal to the country that had offered their ancestors a better life. The United States was enriched in many areas by the influx of so many talented Germans after Hitler came to power. In its 1944 list of prominent scientists, the publication *American Men of Science* included 106 German immigrants. A dozen of these German Americans, who contributed so significantly to American science and education, received Nobel Prizes. Aided by German Americans such as Albert Einstein and Wernher von Braun, America rose to preeminence in science and technology.

A LEGACY OF ACHIEVEMENT

In the twentieth century, the social sciences, literature, medicine, psychoanalysis, film, music, and architecture have all been stimulated by the influx of German talent. An entire German educational institution was transferred to New York as the New School for Social Research. Famous directors, actors, and actresses, such as Marlene Dietrich, went to Hollywood. American music was enriched by Bruno Walter, Otto Klemperer, Arnold Schönberg, and Kurt Weill.

When Hitler closed the Bauhaus, an innovative school for

architecture and design, some of its most imaginative members came to the United States. Walter Gropius at Harvard and Ludwig Mies van der Rohe at the Illinois Institute of Technology influenced a generation of American architects. As Benjamin Franklin said two hundred years ago, "America cultivates best what Germany brought forth."

FAMOUS GERMAN

AMERICANS

Throughout American history, German Americans have made lasting contributions to all aspects of life. Many of these individuals, in fact, have been mentioned in this book. In this chapter, some notable German Americans have been selected, and their achievements in a variety of fields are described.

MILITARY LEADER: FRIEDRICH VON STEUBEN

Friedrich Wilhelm von Steuben was born in Magdeburg, Prussia, on September 17, 1730. Steuben's father was an officer in the Prussian army, and at sixteen he joined as well. He gained the admiration of his king, Frederick the Great, for his performance during the Battle of Rossbach in the Seven Years' War. After the war, he served in the courts of German princes, one of whom gave Steuben the title of baron.

Benjamin Franklin recruited Baron von Steuben to fight in America's revolutionary war. Steuben found dismal conditions and low morale at General Washington's camp at Valley Forge. Though Steuben could speak no English, he won the respect of the men by rising early with them and personally directing their drill. He was able to combine Prussian discipline with frontier tactics to create an effective fighting force of the volunteer patriots.

The regulations that Steuben drew up for the American army were used for decades. Steuben not only transformed the

American army, he became a dedicated American patriot and democrat. In 1779, he wrote, "What a fortunate country this is. . . . I want to die gladly for a nation that has so honored me with its trust." Instead, he lived to see the victorious end of the American struggle.

After the war, General von Steuben became the president of the German Society, which was dedicated to the improvement of the conditions of German immigrants to America. He died on November 25, 1794, in Oneida, New York.

BRAVE IN BATTLE: MOLLY PITCHER

Molly Pitcher, whose real name was Mary Ludwig, was born to German immigrant parents near Trenton, New Jersey, in 1754. As a young girl she worked as a servant at Carlisle, Pennsylvania, in the home of Colonel William Irvine. She later married a young barber, John Casper Hays. John became a gunner in the First Pennsylvania Artillery and spent the winters of 1777 and 1778 at Valley Forge. Mary joined him at the camp and did the cooking, washing, and other chores, and she was with John when the American forces fought the Battle of Monmouth.

The day of the battle, June 28, 1778, was one of the hottest days of the summer, and Mary carried water to the thirsty troops, earning her nickname, "Molly Pitcher." During the battle, her husband suffered a heat stroke. Mary took his place and fought until the end of the battle. She was made a sergeant on the battlefield by General George Washington himself. She died in 1832.

ANNA OTTENDORFER: PUBLISHER

Anna Behr Ottendorfer is another example of a brave and industrious German American. In 1838, she married Jacob Uhl, who later bought a New York newspaper called the *Staatszeitung*. Anna assisted Jacob, and together they developed their newspaper into a daily paper. When her husband died, Anna found time for both her children and the paper, which she continued to manage. She later married Oswald Ottendorfer, who became editor, but she remained business manager of the paper.

With the success of her publishing enterprise, Anna was able to build the Isabella Home for Aged Women in Astoria, Long Island, and the Women's Pavilion of the German Hospital of New York. Anna Ottendorfer's charitable donations were especially significant because she herself had earned all of the money which she donated.

CARL SCHURZ: FIRST SENATOR

Carl Schurz was born in 1829, in Liblar, near Bonn, Germany. As a young man, he joined the liberal wing of the student movement. During the Revolution of 1848, he escaped capture and death by fleeing to Switzerland. He became famous for his courageous return to Germany to rescue his teacher, Professor Gottfried Kinkel, from the Spandau prison.

In London Schurz married Margaretha Meyer, the sister of another refugee from Germany. They sailed to America and settled on a farm in Watertown, Wisconsin. In 1856, Margaretha, influenced by the German educational pioneer Friedrich Fröbel, established the first kindergarten in America.

Carl Schurz joined the new Republican Party and became an abolitionist. At the beginning of the Civil War, he was appointed minister to Spain by President Lincoln. He asked to be recalled and given a military appointment so that he could fight in the war. He commanded a division whose soldiers were mostly German immigrants. After President Lincoln was assassinated, Schurz favored reconciliation with the South. Following the war, he established a German-language newspaper in St. Louis.

In 1869, Schurz was elected to the United States Senate

Carl Schurz

from Missouri, the first German American to hold that office. He served as the secretary of the interior from 1877 to 1881 under President Rutherford B. Hayes and introduced the merit system in the Civil Service. Schurz died in 1906.

CLOTHING PEOPLE: LEVI STRAUSS

Levi Strauss was born in Bavaria in 1829. When he was fourteen, he came to America and lived in Louisville, Kentucky, with an uncle. His brothers, Louis and Jonas, were traders in dry goods in New York. When Levi heard of the discovery of gold in California, he decided to head west. He first went to New York, where he stocked up on silk, cloth, and other luxury items. He also bought a supply of canvas, which was used to make the covers for the Conestoga wagons in which prospectors and pioneers traveled west.

On the way to San Francisco, he sold all of his goods except the canvas. Strauss learned from prospectors that looking for gold was hard on pants, so he had some pants made from canvas. The pants were a sensation and became known as "Levis." In 1853, the Strauss brothers founded a company in New York to make and sell Levi's pants. The brothers soon started making the pants out of another strong cloth, called denim. The pants have remained basically unchanged to this day.

Levi Strauss did not like the term "jeans," and always called his pants overalls. He died in 1902, but his company is still one of the largest manufacturers of pants in the world.

PICTURES AND POLITICS: THOMAS NAST

Thomas Nast was born in Landau in 1840. When he was six years old, his mother brought him to New York. He spent most of his time drawing and, when he was fifteen, got a job doing sketches for *Frank Leslie's Illustrated Newspaper*. He became a famous cartoonist during the Civil War, working for

Harper's Weekly.

Nast was devoted to the Union and to the abolition of slavery. During the Civil War, he drew one of his most famous images, the popular figure of Santa Claus. Some say that Nast looked like his Santa Claus: small, fat, and jolly. He drew two other famous American political symbols, the Democratic donkey and the Republican elephant, which are familiar to many Americans today.

Nast used his cartoons to fight corruption. Some of his most famous cartoons targeted the corrupt politician Boss Tweed of New York City, who, along with his followers, had been robbing the city for years. One of Nast's drawings of Tweed was recognized by the police in Italy, where Tweed had fled, and he was arrested.

President Ulysses S. Grant was a friend of Nast, and President Theodore Roosevelt appointed him consul to Ecuador. On December 7, 1902, Nast died there.

TIME AND SPACE: ALBERT EINSTEIN

Albert Einstein was born on March 14, 1879, in Ulm. Despite the fact that he did not do well in mathematics as a young student, he became one of the most important mathematicians and scientists of modern times. His "general theory of relativity," developed in 1915, was a revolutionary departure in physics and in many ways laid the basis for our current understanding of the way the universe works. He won the Nobel Prize in 1921 for theoretical physics and his work in photoelectricity.

In 1933, Einstein gave up his membership in the Prussian Academy and his German citizenship because of the anti-Semitic policies of the Nazi government. He moved to Princeton, New Jersey. There he became the director of mathematics at Princeton's Institute for Advanced Studies. His warning about German scientific developments prompted

Albert Einstein

President Franklin Delano Roosevelt to initiate the Manhattan Project to construct an atomic bomb. Einstein did not participate in this program, but his scientific work directly contributed to its success.

After the war, Einstein was an outspoken advocate of world peace and cooperation. He died in Princeton on March 18, 1955.

CANADIAN IDENTITY: JOHN DIEFENBAKER

John George Diefenbaker was born in Neustadt, Ontario, on September 18, 1895. His father had come to Canada from Germany, where he had married a woman of Scottish descent. Young John grew up on the prairies of Saskatchewan and earned a master's degree from the University of Saskatchewan. He served in the Canadian army during World War I. He earned a law degree after returning from France and became the first lawyer in his family.

Although Diefenbaker lost his first five campaigns for public office, he remained undiscouraged. He ran for the Canadian House of Commons in 1940. That time he won. In Parliament, he was a champion of civil rights and the Canadian identity. He proposed that Canadians become citizens of Canada rather than of Great Britain. He also advocated the removal of the indication of national origin from the citizenship records of Canadians. He wanted all inhabitants of Canada to be regarded as Canadians.

There had not been a Conservative Party prime minister since 1935, but in 1957 Diefenbaker changed this when he became the first Canadian prime minister of neither British nor French ancestry. During his tenure, a program of national health insurance was enacted. His party lost its majority in 1963, when he refused to allow atomic warheads to be placed on United States missiles stationed in Canada. He was replaced as leader of the Progressive Conservative Party in 1967, but he continued to serve in parliament until his death on August 16, 1979.

DIPLOMACY: HENRY KISSINGER

Heinz Alfred Kissinger was born in Fürth, Germany, on May 27, 1923. He grew up in an orthodox Jewish family. After Hitler came to power, Kissinger's father lost his job and the family became refugees from Nazi persecution. In 1938,

Dr. Henry Kissinger, while on a diplomatic mission to China, is met at the airport by dignitaries.

they went to New York.

Heinz changed his name to Henry and began working in a factory and going to night school at City College. He was drafted into the army. After the defeat of Germany, he served as an administrator with the American military government in its sector of occupied Germany. In 1946, he returned to America and went to Harvard College on a scholarship from the state of New York.

At Harvard, Kissinger majored in government and was

elected to the academic honors society Phi Beta Kappa. He earned his Ph.D. in 1954. He became executive director of Harvard's foreign student project, which later became the Harvard International Seminar. He served as an adviser to Presidents Eisenhower, Kennedy, and Johnson. In 1969, President Nixon appointed him Assistant to the President for National Security Affairs. Under Kissinger, the National Security Council became a major force in American foreign policy. He was appointed secretary of state in 1973. Also in 1973, Kissinger was awarded the Nobel Peace Prize for his role in ending the war in Vietnam.

TIME LINE

1683	Mennonites led by Francis Pastorius, a thirty-two-year-old lawyer from Frankfurt, settle in Germantown, near Philadelphia, Pennsylvania.
1688	The Germantown Mennonites draw up the first protest in America against the enslavement of Africans.
1689	Jacob Leisler, a soldier and trader from Frankfurt, is chosen by the common people to be governor of New York; in 1691 he is executed by his conservative British opponents, becoming America's first martyr to democracy.
1709	Germans from the Palatinate along the Rhine River, fleeing the destruction caused by the invading French, emigrate to the Hudson River Valley and Pennsylvania.
1710	Another group of Palatine Germans settles New Bern, North Carolina.
1714	Christopher Dock, who introduced the use of the blackboard into American schools, begins teaching in Pennsylvania.
1732	Benjamin Franklin begins publishing a newspaper in German, the *Philadelphische Zeitung*.
1733	Johann Peter Rockefeller arrives in America to work on a farm and becomes the founder of the famous American business family.
1733	John Peter Zenger, champion of freedom of the press, founds his *New York Weekly Journal*.
1734	Refugees from Salzburg arrive in Savannah, Georgia.
1743	Christopher Saur II prints the first Bible in the English colonies, in German.
1750	The first Germans arrive in Nova Scotia.
1750	Gottlieb Mittelberger writes his *Journey to Pennsylvania*, which reports the horrors experienced by immigrants sailing from Germany to America.
1753	Hanoverians found the town of Lunenburg, which will become the most important ship-building center of Nova Scotia.

1754	The Schwenfelders of Pennsylvania establish the first Sunday school in America.
1756-1763	Germans play a significant role in fighting the French in the French and Indian War.
1773	German states, concerned over the loss of working people, regulate and limit the activities of recruiters of emigrants.
1776	The U.S. Continental Congress authorizes the recruitment of a German regiment in Pennsylvania and Maryland.
1777	A cavalry unit composed of Germans and commanded by Major Friedrich von Heer serves as General George Washington's bodyguard.
1778	General Friedrich William von Steuben becomes the Inspector General of the Revolutionary Army.
1783	German Loyalists settle in Upper Canada, where the town of Berlin, changed to Kitchener during World War I, will become the center of a predominantly German area.
1784	The Deutsche Gesellschaft is founded in New York to assist new German immigrants.
1787	Franklin College is established in Lancaster, Pennsylvania, as a German-language educational institution.
1789	Frederick Augustus Mühlenberg becomes the first Speaker of the U.S. House of Representatives.
1798	Germans in Pennsylvania resist the Alien and Sedition Laws.
1799	Pennsylvania Germans join Fries' Rebellion against direct federal property taxes.
1808	George Michael Bedinger, a Kentucky pioneer whose parents were born in Germany, authors a bill that prohibits the importation of slaves into the United States.
1819	The U.S. Congress passes the Passenger Act, ending the redemptioner trade.
1828	Discriminatory laws against Jews in Bavaria and Württemberg lead to the immigration of many merchants to the southern United States.
1829	In Germany, Gottfried Duden publishes accounts of his experiences on a farm in Missouri; his idealized depiction of life in America encourages more Germans to emigrate.
1835	The *Anzeiger des Westens*, the first German newspaper in St. Louis, is established; the next year, the first German-English school west of the Mississippi is also established in St. Louis.

1837　Laws in Pennsylvania and Ohio permit public school to be conducted in German.

1839　Theodore Bernhard, a German American, initiates a free textbook program in Wisconsin.

1842　The Zentralverein is organized to give German Catholics an alternative to Masonic lodges.

1844　The Adelsverein begins a program to settle Germans in Texas.

1845　Hermann Kriege founds the first German-American labor organization, the Bund der Gerichten, in New York.

1846　Crop failures in Germany, followed by foreclosures, encourage more Germans to emigrate to America.

1847　The Missouri Synod of the Lutheran Church is organized in protest against Americanization and liberalization of the Lutheran Church in America.

1848　Political refugees flee Germany when democratic revolutions there fail.

1848　The Germania Orchestra is founded in New York.

1849　Dr. Abraham Jacobi establishes the first free children's clinic in the United States.

1850　The first *Turnverein* (Turner Hall) in the United States opens in Cincinnati.

1850　Bloody clashes begin between anti-foreign nativists, or "Know-Nothings," and German Americans begin and continue throughout the decade.

1851　Emmanuel Leutze paints *Washington Crossing the Delaware* for the U.S. Capitol building.

1854　Germans hold mass meetings in many American cities to protest the repeal of the Missouri Compromise and the extension of slavery through the Kansas-Nebraska Act.

1855　Heinrich Steinweg, the founder of the Steinway piano company, arrives in America.

1856　The first kindergarten in the United States is organized by Margaretha Meyer Schurz in Watertown, Wisconsin.

1861　Union forces in Missouri, consisting mostly of German militia, play a significant role in keeping that state in the Union.

1861　Nine German Americans hold the rank of major general in the Union Army.

1869　Carl Schurz is elected U.S. Senator from Missouri, the first German-born citizen to become a member of the Senate.

1870- German Americans hail the defeat of France in the Franco-
1871   Prussian War and the unification of Germany on January 18,
       1871.

1873   The St. Louis School Board makes kindergarten part of its
       public school system.

1874   The migration of German-speaking Mennonites from Russia to
       the prairies of Manitoba begins.

1877   Carl Schurz becomes secretary of the interior in President
       Rutherford B. Hayes' cabinet.

1884   Leopold Damrosch, a German-born musician and conductor,
       begins the first season of German opera at the Metropolitan
       Opera House in New York.

1887   August Spies, the editor of the Chicago *Arbeiter-Zeitung*, and
       seven other Germans are executed for inciting labor protests that
       resulted in the 1886 Haymarket Riot.

1890   Victor Berger of the Socialist Party is elected mayor of
       Milwaukee.

1914– German-American organizations attempt to prevent the United
1917   States from supporting Great Britain in World War I.

1917   Germans suffer a wave of anti-German sentiment after the
       United States declares war on Germany.

1918   Hutterites migrate from the United States to the prairies of
       Canada.

1919   The Steuben Society is organized by German Americans to
       promote Americanization and to combat attacks on German
       Americans.

1920's After the anti-German emotions stirred by the war have
       diminished, many German skilled workers and technicians
       migrate to Canada to work in the industrial centers of Ontario.

1933   Adolf Hitler becomes Chancellor of Germany; his intensifying
       anti-Semitic campaign drives many German Jews to seek refuge
       in the United States, but U.S. quotas imposed in 1929 limit the
       number allowed into the country.

1936   The pro-Hitler German-American Bund and the American Nazi
       Party attract the support of only a small percentage of German
       Americans.

1942   General Dwight D. Eisenhower, whose German ancestors settled
       in Texas, becomes the commander of the U.S. forces in Europe.

1945   American forces participate in the occupation of defeated Germany.

1948   The Marshall Plan makes U.S. financial assistance available to Germany, enabling it to recuperate from the ravages of World War II.

1948   The Displaced Persons Act allows additional ethnic Germans, expelled from Eastern Europe, to immigrate to America.

1949   With the support of the United States, the Federal Republic of Germany is organized in West Germany.

1950's   Approximately 250,000 Germans, many of them skilled workers, migrate to the cities of Canada.

1957   John Diefenbaker, a descendant of German immigrants, becomes the first Canadian prime minister to come from the non-British, non-French population of Canada.

1961   The Berlin Wall is erected by the Communist regime in East Germany to cut off immigration to the West.

1989   The hard-line regime in East Germany collapses and the Berlin Wall is opened.

1990   On October 3, the German Democratic Republic (East Germany) joins the Federal Republic of Germany (West Germany), thus again uniting Germany, which had been divided as a result of World War II.

GLOSSARY

Amish: The Protestant religious sect whose members shun modern conveniences and maintain a simple, austere lifestyle.

Anschluss: German for "union" or "junction." This name is applied to the forced annexation of Austria by Adolf Hitler's Germany in March, 1938.

Auf Wiedersehen: German for "until we see each other again," or "good-bye for now." This common German farewell is sometimes used by English speakers.

Beer garden: A gathering place in which German Americans could socialize, dance, and sing, and where German beer and food were typically consumed.

Blitz: From German for "lightning." A rapid military attack.

Bratwurst: A white pork sausage, common in the Midwest and elsewhere in North America where German-American communities are concentrated.

Braunschweiger: Liver sausage.

Bruderhofs: The réligious communities of the Hutterites, who believe in sharing property.

Damenverein: A German women's society.

Dunkers: From German *tunken*, "to dunk." Members of a dissenting religious group which stressed baptism by immersion, or dunking under water.

Fasching: The German pre-Lenten carnival celebration.

Frankfurter: A hot dog. It is named after the city of Frankfurt, where a forerunner of this sausage was eaten in Germany.

Fräulein: A young, unmarried woman.

Gemeinschaft: German for "society." A group of people organized in a contractual agreement.

Gemütlichkeit: An atmosphere or feeling of geniality, cozy comfort, and shared good times.

Gesangverein: A German singing club.

Gesundheit: German for "health." A word typically said to a person who has sneezed.

Hamburger: A ground-meat patty named after a German dish from Hamburg, Germany.

Hutterites: Followers of the Anabaptist Christian reformer, Jacob Hutter. They lead simple lives, oppose violence and war, and believe in the common ownership of property.

Kaffeeklatsch: An informal party or gathering with coffee and pastries.

Kindergarten: From the German words meaning "children's garden." A preschool for young children. Margaretha Meyer Schurz transplanted this German educational innovation to America.

Liverwurst: The English-language equivalent of German *Leberwurst*, a sausage made of ground liver.

Mennonites: Christians, inspired by the reformer Menno Simons, who oppose infant baptism, the taking of oaths, and military service. They dress and live simply.

Nazism: The political movement of Adolf Hitler, the German dictator from 1933 to 1945. Nazis were anti-Semitic.

Oktoberfest: A autumn harvest festival celebrated in Bavaria.

Pennsylvania Dutch: Another name for those German Americans who originally settled in Pennsylvania.

Polka: An energetic German dance.

Prosit: A German toast borrowed from the Latin meaning "To your health!"

Putsch: The German equivalent of a *coup d'état*, or overthrow of a government.

Realpolitik: A politics of realism or a policy brutally calculated to achieve one's objectives.

Redemptioner: An indentured servant, a person who gave up his or her rights for a time in return for the cost of travel to America.

Sauerkraut: From German for "sour cabbage." Chopped, salted cabbage that has been allowed to ferment.

Schnitzel: A veal cutlet.

Stein: Short for German *Steinkrug*, or "stone jug." An earthenware or glass beer mug.

Strudel: A thin pastry covering fruit or cheese.

Torte: A cake containing thin layers of custard, fruit, or chocolate.

Turnverein: A German fraternal organization. Founded in Germany in the early 1800's by Friedrich Jahn, such athletic and gymnastic societies were intended to foster German patriotism and nationalism.

Unterstützungsverein: A German aid society. Such societies assisted German immigrants in the early 1800's, often acting as insurance agencies.

Verboten: Forbidden, taboo.

Volksdeutsche: People of German culture who lived outside Germany in eastern Europe.

Waltz: From the German for "roll." A German and Austrian dance performed in three-quarter time. When first introduced, it was frowned upon by Puritans because it encouraged dance partners to dance close together.

Wanderlust: Restlessness; a strong desire to travel.

Weltanschauung: German for "worldview." A comprehensive view of life or human history.

Wiener: A hot dog. In German, "Wienerwurst" means a sausage typical of Vienna (Wien), Austria.

Wunderbar: German for "wonderful." Used in English to mean the same.

RESOURCES

American Council on Germany
14 E. 60th St.
New York, NY 10022
   This group works to improve understanding between the United States and Germany by providing opportunities for young German and American professionals to exchange ideas and experiences.

American Historical Society of Germans from Russia
631 D. St.
Lincoln, NE 68502
   This organization of persons of German-Russian ancestry encourages research and the preservation of the history of Germans from Russia. It assists people of German-Russian ancestry with their genealogical research and maintains a library, museum, and archives. Among the activities it sponsors are annual workshops in folklore, genealogy, religious history, translation, research, and bibliography.

German American National Congress
4740 N. Western Ave., 2d Floor
Chicago, IL 60625
   The German American National Congress has thirty thousand members of German ancestry. It is a nonpartisan civic organization that attempts to preserve German culture, art, and customs and promote the study of German in American schools.

German Information Center
410 Park Ave.
New York, NY 10022
   The German Information Center provides educational material to teachers and other interested persons. Its publication *Information: The Federal Republic of German and the USA* lists German archives and other useful information.

German Society of Pennsylvania
611 Spring Garden Rd.
Philadelphia, PA 19123

This organization encourages the understanding of German and German-American culture and history through its library, educational programs, and social activities. It sponsors lectures, exhibits, and concerts. It also offers courses in German and gives awards to high school students for proficiency in German.

Germans-from-Russia Heritage Society
1008 E. Central Ave.
Bismarck, ND 58501

The society's members are persons interested in preserving the heritage of Germans who came to America from Russia. The organization preserves genealogical records and operates a surname exchange. It has archives and encourages members to write their family histories. Local groups sponsor Oktoberfests, heritage days, food festivals, songfests, and lectures.

North American Singers Association
6236 N. Kildare Ave.
Chicago, IL 60646

This is a group of active singers belonging to German-American choruses. It promotes pride in German-American heritage and tradition, sponsoring competitions and granting awards and prizes. It could provide information concerning the location of German-American choruses in specific locales.

Pennsylvania German Society
P.O. Box 397
Birdsboro, PA 19508

This society consists of descendants of German pioneers who settled in Pennsylvania or other colonies, as well as other people interested in collecting and preserving the records of the Pennsylvania Dutch. It encourages the preservation of this history.

Steuben Society of America
67-05 Fresh Pond Rd.
Ridgewood, NY 11385

The Steuben Society was founded in 1919 to promote the Americanization of German Americans, to foster American patriotism, and to encourage participation of German Americans in public affairs. It publishes *The Steuben News,* which underlines the contributions made to American culture by Americans of German heritage. American citizens of German extraction can join.

BIBLIOGRAPHY

Conzen, Kathleen Neils. *Immigrant Milwaukee, 1836-1860: Accommodation and Community in a Frontier City.* Cambridge, Mass.: Harvard University Press, 1976. A study of early German immigration to Milwaukee by the author of the entry "Germans" in the *Harvard Encyclopedia of American Ethnic Groups.* Conzen illustrates the whole texture of German immigrant life, including patterns of arrival, family characteristics, and economic activity. The summaries at the end of each chapter should be particularly useful to young readers.

Cunz, Dieter. *The Maryland Germans: A History.* Princeton, N.J.: Princeton University Press, 1948. A carefully researched and interesting book, which covers reasons for immigration, the immigrants' way of life, and the process of amalgamation.

Faust, Albert Bernhard. *The German Element in the United States.* 2 vols. New York: Steuben Society of America, 1927. First published in 1909, these two volumes provide detailed treatment of colonial and nineteenth century German immigration and German-American culture during that period.

Keil, Hartmut, ed. *German Workers' Culture in the United States, 1850-1920.* Washington, D.C.: Smithsonian Institution Press, 1988. The articles in this volume are by scholars of German-American working-class society and culture. Excellent for teachers and advanced students.

Mittelberger, Gottlieb. *Journey to Pennsylvania.* Edited and translated by Oscar Handlin and John Clive. Cambridge, Mass.: Harvard University Press, 1960. A translation of the fascinating account by a young German immigrant in the eighteenth century of his trip across the Atlantic and his experiences in Pennsylvania. Appropriate for middle school and beyond.

Peck, Abraham J., ed. *The German-Jewish Legacy in America, 1938-1988.* Detroit: Wayne State University Press, 1989. A collection of essays on the twentieth century German-Jewish community in America.

Rippley, La Vern J. *The German Americans.* Lanham: University Press of America, 1984. A comprehensive study of the German Americans, first published in 1976. It contains extensive treatment of German-American culture and society and is filled with facts concerning particular Germans and their contributions.

Tolzmann, Don Heinrich. *The Cincinnati Germans After the Great War.* New York: Peter Lang, 1987. Despite its title, this book effectively tells the pre-World War I story of the German experience in Cincinnati, as well as the tragic impact of that war upon the German-American community. Highly recommended for advanced students.

Trommler, Frank, and Joseph McVeigh, eds. *America and the Germans: An Assessment of a Three-Hundred-Year History.* 2 vols. Philadelphia: University of Pennsylvania Press, 1985. The most up-to-date compilation of scholarship on the German Americans, these two volumes provide a lively study of the German experience in America from the colonial period to the present.

Wittke, Carl F. *Refugees of Revolution: The German Forty-Eighters in America.* Philadelphia: University of Pennsylvania, 1952. Wittke considers the influence of these immigrants on the Germans already in America and upon American life in general. Wittke emphasizes the most prominent of these individuals but provides an array of names and incidents. This scholarly work is recommended for teachers and advanced students.

Wood, Ralph. *The Pennsylvania Germans.* Princeton, N.J.: Princeton University Press, 1942. A scholarly treatment of the origin of the German community in Pennsylvania and its social and cultural characteristics. Wood discusses farming, religious sects, and education in this delightful book.

MEDIA BIBLIOGRAPHY

VIDEOCASSETTES

The Dream Spinner: A Film Saga of the Germans in Missouri.
Videocassette with study guide. Directed by David J. McAllister.
Missouri Committee for the Humanities, 4144 Lindell Blvd., St. Louis,
MO 63108, and the Max Kade Foundation.

The Germans in Gretna. Videocassette. Gretna Historical Society, Huey P.
Long Ave., Gretna, LA 70053. A history of the German community in
the Gretna area of greater New Orleans.

Where Have All the Germans Gone? Videocassette, 52 minutes.
Distributed by Media Guild, 11526 Sorrento Valley Rd., Suite J, San
Diego, CA 92121. One in the Destination America series, produced by
Thames Television.

TELEVISION

Benson. In this situation comedy, Inga Swenson plays Gretchen Kraus,
the rigid and authoritarian German housekeeper of a governor's
mansion.

Centennial. A 1978-1979 mini-series based on the novel of the same name
by James A. Michener. Raymond Burr plays the German settler,
Hermann Bockweiss; Alex Karras plays Hans Brumbaugh; and
Gregory Harrison plays the Pennsylvania Dutch settler Levi Zendt.

Little House on the Prairie. Although the Ingalls family portrayed in this
series is Scandinavian, Almanzo Wilder, who eventually marries Laura,
is portrayed as a German American (as suggested by Laura Ingalls
Wilder's book *Farmer Boy*). German farming families are featured in a
number of the *Little House* episodes.

Hogan's Heroes. A situation comedy in which the Nazi antagonist,
Colonel Klink, is head of a German prisoner-of-war camp during
World War II. This unflattering caricature is less offensive than the
comic approach to the Nazis, which humanizes them and therefore (if
unintentionally) makes light of their crimes.

NOVELS

Alcott, Louisa May. *Little Women*, 1868. Alcott's novel is a largely autobiographical sentimental romance set in a New England village, New York City, and Italy. The story is about three sisters, one of whom, Jo, eventually marries a lovable and eccentric German immigrant, Professor Bhaer. Together, they open a boys' school, which is explored in the sequel to the novel, *Little Men.*

Kafka, Franz. *Amerika*, 1927. This novel was written between 1912 and 1914 by one of the most important writers of the twentieth century. Karl Rossmann, the book's protagonist, is buffeted by the unpredictability of life in America, to which he immigrated with great expectations. He is unable to deal with the gap between the myth of America and the reality of the early twentieth century in American society.

Michener, James A. *Centennial*, 1975. This novel provides a panoramic treatment of the settlement of the West. Key characters are German immigrants and a Pennsylvania Dutch family, who settle in Colorado.

Solger, Reinhold. *Anton in America: Novelle aus dem deutsch-amerikanischen Leben*, 1872. Published in New York, this novel (literally, "Anton in America: A Novel About the German-American experience") became the best-known prose piece published in German in the United States. It was, for Germans, one of the main sources of information about life in the United States.

Stein, Gertrude. *The Gentle Lena*, 1909. This is the third of the women covered in Stein's series entitled *Three Lives*. Lena is a German immigrant brought to America by her aunt. The aunt secures a job for Lena as a servant and eventually arranges a marriage for her. Stein stresses the alienation of the simple Lena. Stein takes care to use German-American idiom in the story, which makes this novel particularly interesting.

Suckow, Ruth. *Country People*, 1924. Suckow, herself a descendant of Germans, provides a record of the German settlers of her native Iowa. During the lifetime of the main characters, August Kätterhenry, the Iowa frontier prospers and the German-American farmers are assimilated.

MOTION PICTURES

Alice in the Cities (*Alice in den Städten*), 1974. This film by director Wim Wenders tells the story of a German journalist searching first for a story in New York City and along the East Coast and then for a young girls' grandmother in Europe. The friendship between the eight-year-old Alice and the journalist is the heart of the film.

The American Friend, 1977. Another film by Wim Wenders, exploring the relationship between an American, an international art dealer who sells fake artwork, and a German restorer of paintings. Themes concern identity and rootlessness. The plot is set in New York, Paris, and Germany.

The American Soldier (Der amerikanische Soldat), 1970. Directed by Rainer Werner Fassbinder, this film is the story of an American Vietnam veteran whose ancestors were German immigrants to the United States. He goes to Munich as a hired killer.

Bagdad Café, 1988. Tells the story of the relationship between Jasmin, a German woman who was touring the United States with her husband before he abandoned her. She meets Brenda, the owner of a run-down truck stop and motel in an American desert town. Originally at odds with each other, the two become close friends and make a success of the diner, bringing joy back into the lives of the locals. Directed by Peter Adlon.

The Emperor of California (Der Kaiser von Kalifornien), 1937. This 1937 film by Luis Trenker tells the story of John Augustus Sutter, a German immigrant who was granted land in California on which gold was discovered. Sutter later became a U.S. senator and a general in the U.S. army. Regarded by many as the best German-made western.

Stroszek, 1977. This film by Werner Herzog chronicles the immigration of the former prisoner Stroszek and Eva to America, and their sorrowful ending in the "land of plenty."

Witness, 1985. Australian director Peter Weir depicts the Amish of Pennsylvania and a challenge to their traditional ways, posed by a detective investigating a murder. The violence and alienation of modern America are contrasted with the simplicity and sense of the community of the Amish.

MUSIC

Germans brought a rich musical tradition with them to America. In the nineteenth century, they organized groups to perform the music of Johann Sebastian Bach, Ludwig van Beethoven, and Wolfgang Amadeus Mozart. In the later nineteenth century, Johannes Brahms gained a prominent place in the German-American repertoire. Two favorites of the German

Americans were Schiller's *An die Friede* (*Hymn to Joy*), used by Beethoven in his Ninth Symphony, and George Frideric Handel's *Messiah*. German folk songs, many of which were sung by German Americans, are available on a number of records. Among them are *Best-Loved Folk Songs* (in German), on the Monitor label (MFS-389); *Drinking Songs* (in German), again on the Monitor label (MFS-399); *I Love the Music of a German Beer Hall*, on Nesak (19402-2); and *Oktoberfest im Hofbrauhaus*, on Fiesta (1626). Other recordings include:

Dietrich, Marlene. *Wiedersehen mit Marlene.* A recording of the singing of the famous actress who emigrated from Germany in 1930, from Capitol records.

Kollo, René. *Kollo Sings Favorite German Folk Songs*, from Koch Records International, and *Der Tenor und seine Lieder* (the tenor and his songs), on the Acanta label. These recordings provide quality renditions of German songs. The latter album includes the favorites "Edelweiss," "Rosemarie," and "Still wie die Nacht," or "Silent Night."

Trapp Family Singers. *Best of the Trapp Family Singers* and *Christmas with the Trapp Family Singers*. The Trapp family fled Austria after the Anschluss and traveled to America. These recordings are available from MCA and provide many examples of German and Austrian songs.

INDEX